R Smith

THE
MOST
PROBABLE
WORLD

SOME BOOKS BY STUART CHASE

✩

THE MOST PROBABLE WORLD

MONEY TO GROW ON

AMERICAN CREDOS

LIVE AND LET LIVE

SOME THINGS WORTH KNOWING

GUIDES TO STRAIGHT THINKING

THE PROPER STUDY OF MANKIND

POWER OF WORDS

ROADS TO AGREEMENT

DEMOCRACY UNDER PRESSURE

WHERE'S THE MONEY COMING FROM?

THE TYRANNY OF WORDS

RICH LAND, POOR LAND

A NEW DEAL

THE ECONOMY OF ABUNDANCE

MEXICO

MEN AND MACHINES

YOUR MONEY'S WORTH (WITH F. J. SCHLINK)

THE TRAGEDY OF WASTE

STUART CHASE

THE

☆

MOST

☆

PROBABLE

☆

WORLD

HARPER & ROW, PUBLISHERS

NEW YORK, EVANSTON, AND LONDON

CONTENTS

FOREWORD

SOME men in the United States and Russia are headed for the moon. They confidently expect to walk around on its surface in their space suits before the decade is out. Then they will head hopefully back to earth. Other men, not many, are wondering if they can walk around on Mars, but with a longer journey there and back. Few men who know anything about physics and astronomy expect ever to walk around outside the solar system.

Where are the rest of us earthlings headed? What fate is in store for us; what is the most probable world here on earth?

I have been thinking about this book for a long time. I have thought about some of its issues ever since I began to write. It has given me a chance to return to some subjects I have studied earlier and to update them—and to see how wrong I was in one particular or another. The chapter on the conservation of living space follows—at a considerable distance—my book *Rich Land, Poor Land*. The chapter on the mixed economy describes a trend that I began to sense in *Government in Business* (1935), and have emphasized in other studies, most recently in *Money to Grow On*. My interest in the impact of technology on the human condition—stimulated perhaps by undergraduate years at the Massachusetts Institute of Technology—was documented first in *Men and Machines,* later in

The Economy of Abundance, and in many articles and reviews. The necessity for extending the scientific method to
improve our understanding of human nature was the subject
of a book on the social sciences which is used as background
reading in many universities and is widely translated abroad—
The Proper Study of Mankind.

I can remember as a small boy the first electric light installed in my grandfather's house in New England, and the
first automobile on the street outside, and I have recently
watched on television a space capsule with men aboard coming down on target in the ocean, to be picked up by helicopter.
"In the span of less than a single lifetime," says Dr. Leland
Haworth, director of the National Science Foundation, "virtually every aspect of our society and our personal lives has
been vitally affected by the tremendous impact of science and
technology." He could have gone further and noted that without this impact most of us now alive would never have been
born. The population of the world—with a death rate of up-
wards of 40 per thousand, instead of the present 10—would
still be less than a billion, rather than the present three billion
and a third.

That I have lived through this era of shattering change is
one qualification for trying to predict its future course. Another is that I want the truest picture I can get of the world
outside my head, and am intensely curious about its direction.

You will find a good many facts in the following pages, but
this is not a reference book. I have tried to hold facts and
figures to the point of establishing a trend beyond challenge,
without bringing in all the relevant data. While the trends,
furthermore, are world-wide, affecting all cultures, the most
reliable statistics are to be found in high-energy societies, and
the readiest at hand for me apply to the United States.

Technology is enforcing changes so rapidly that one must

write as he runs. Some of the material will certainly be outdated in due course, and much of it comes from the daily *New York Times,* in stories breaking before the data have appeared in solid books. This is particularly true of the twin trends toward the arms race—say antimissile missiles, and toward one world—say the next phase in the United Nations, following the war in the Near East. It is quite impossible, furthermore, to keep up with the electronic computer. For example, there are three new uses, all important, in the *Times* this morning as I write.

Although I am seeking to project into the future trends which seem urgent, this study is no crystal ball undertaking. Other writers have raked their imaginations in an attempt to picture what the condition of man will be in 1984, or at the end of the twentieth century, or a hundred years, a thousand years, from now. One of the world's most daring imaginers, Olaf Stapledon in *Last and First Men,* takes a fix on the year A.D. two billion, after 15 varieties of sentient beings—including a species which makes a mass migration to Neptune—have come and gone. His is the longest view of Homo sapiens I know of. H. G. Wells, in *Men Like Gods,* transferred three automobile loads of present-day earthlings to a planet, out beyond Sirius, with similar physical conditions to our own, using a massive equation of relativity to get them there.

We class these fancies as Utopias, following Sir Thomas More, who wrote the first *Utopia* in Latin in 1516. Most picture an ideal culture, where sin and war and poverty have been outgrown. Bellamy's *Looking Backward* is a classic example. Other visions, such as Orwell's *1984* and Huxley's *Brave New World,* are, by contrast, pretty grim, with citizens suffering under brutal commissars and expert brainwashers.

Obviously this present book is not in the Utopian tradition —except for one lyrical passage, carefully segregated in the epilogue. It takes a hardheaded look at ten current trends, all deriving from science since Galileo, and then attempts to project them into the next few decades, say to the year 2000. What do they promise for the human condition? What might be the resultant of these powerful forces?

Here, of course, I am compelled to use my imagination like any writer of Utopias, but there is very little that is imaginative about the description of the trends. The fact that the population of the world will double by the end of the century at the present rate of growth cannot seriously be challenged. No competent demographer doubts it. Nor can one deny that an all-out nuclear exchange today would end both the United States and Russia as viable societies. The curve which shows the bulk of inanimate energy coming from atomic power plants by the year 2000—assuming no nuclear war—cannot be seriously doubted.

My title, *The Most Probable World,* can be doubted, and I hope readers will vigorously debate it. The more minds that begin to think seriously about where we are headed, the better. H. Bentley Glass, professor of biology, states the case forcibly:

If we are going to develop a civilization broadly and soundly based upon scientific foundations—and we can hardly escape that now—every citizen, every man in the street must learn what science truly is, and what risks and quandaries, as well as what magnificent gifts, the powers that grow out of scientific discovery engender.[1]

Anatol Rapoport, professor of mathematical biology, and a leading student of semantics, points out that there are two kinds of probability: the rigorously mathematical and the more subjective "degree of belief." The first has to do with the frequency of an event: e.g., the probability of number four recurring in a throw of dice. Scientific probabilities, he says,

[1] *Science and Ethical Values.* This and other useful works can be found in the Reading List, p. 231.

He didn't say this.

go back to this. But there are no frequencies to count and measure in probability as a "degree of belief." When C. P. Snow said that a nuclear bomb would go off within ten years he was using the second definition. There have not been enough such explosions in active warfare upon which to calculate a frequency.

This study partakes of both kinds of probability, but the conclusions certainly lean on the second, namely, a degree of belief. Here are the trends, reasonably well documented, and here is where I believe they are taking us. I cannot prove, indeed nobody can prove, that the resultant will be thus and so in five years, or 35.

Scanning the headlines in this summer of 1967—riots in Detroit and other cities, war in Vietnam, the Middle East, China, Nigeria—it seems clear enough that Homo sapiens is largely unprepared for the most probable world. In this book I try to outline some tentative preparation. The ten trends described in the chapters to come all derive from modern science and technology. They are dynamic, and are bound to affect man's future over and above his several preferences and ideologies. It may not be too strong to call them jointly the *technological imperative.*

material / nonmaterial (?)

Galbraith tech. imp.

If Homo sapiens can become aware of these trends and work with them, his chances for survival and even for the good life should be improved. If you ask me what I think are the chances for such adaptation, I can only reply that if I did not believe the chances to be better than even, I would hardly have wasted my time documenting the end of the human story.

In the foreword to *Last and First Men,* Olaf Stapledon acknowledges the "devastating sanity" of his wife in helping with the manuscript. A similar quality in my wife, Marian, has helped me, and so has her curiosity about the psychological impact of technology. I am grateful to William Karraker, Evan Thomas, Cass Canfield, and Norbert Slepyan for many

FOREWORD

helpful suggestions, and to Dorothy Rutherford for her excellent secretarial help.

STUART CHASE

Redding, Connecticut
September, 1967

✭

". . . one must either anticipate change or be its victim."

JOHN KENNETH GALBRAITH

"The great hope for the future, as in the past, lies in the fact of change. The question is not whether history is moving in the direction of sparing modern man from nuclear incineration, but whether modern man can recognize auspicious change when he sees it."

NORMAN COUSINS

"We of today must conceive our relations to the rest of the universe as best we can; and even if our images must seem fantastic to future men, they may none the less serve their purpose today."

W. OLAF STAPLEDON

"A society that blindly accepts the decisions of experts is a sick society. The time has come when we must produce, alongside specialists, another class of scholars and citizens who have broad familiarity with the facts, methods and objectives of science and are thus capable of making judgments about scientific policies . . . persons who work at the interface of science and society have become essential."

RENÉ DUBOS

"For every advancement in science causes a displacement in society, which in turn calls for new inventions with further displacements. The process is one of geometric progression. This is the fundamental nature of the revolution caused by modern science, the greatest happening in all history."

JAMES T. SHOTWELL

THE

MOST

PROBABLE

WORLD

☆

1

IT BEGAN WITH GALILEO

IS Western technology a juggernaut riding over us and depressing the human spirit or carrying us to Doomsday? We have heard such questions so often that many of us have shut our ears to them. Nevertheless, there the questions are, and if we want to discern even a vague picture of the world our children will have to live in, we must try to trace what we are doing to our planet, and what technology in turn is doing to us. But first, we need at least a rough account of how the trends that shape our culture began, and an estimate of where they may take us tomorrow.

Leonardo da Vinci tried to invent a device which would permit a man to fly. There are men alive today who can remember their elders saying, "Thus far and no farther; flying is impossible." What would Leonardo make of an astronaut circling the earth in a metal cylinder at 18,000 miles an hour; then stepping out into nothingness to view the great illuminated globe hundreds of miles below? Have men become gods? No—hardly gods. But in space research some men have developed enough to command perhaps the full potential of the human brain. Whether they have the judgment, experience, and perspective to make wise decisions about human problems is another question.

It all began with Galileo. He laid down the principles of the

1

scientific method, whereby the findings of one competent observer can be checked by another and yet another, until an
objective, impersonal nugget of truth is established. Before
Galileo, conclusions were arrived at by verbal logic and intui-
tion, and were not subject to verification in the laboratory or
the field. Such methods of seeking knowledge—philosophical,
theological, or intuitive—may rise to great popular heights,
but presently they decline. Theologians are today debating,
with no little publicity, the question "Is God dead?" But science, as inaugurated by Galileo, goes on with one dependable
finding laid upon another in an ever-mounting body of
verifiable knowledge.

Using this method, Kepler deduced certain laws governing
the behavior of heavenly bodies. A century later, Newton used
the same method to work out the basic laws of motion and
gravity. Einstein, two centuries later again, recast Newton's
findings in a grander frame of reference. All this was accomplished by using the earth as a platform from which to observe
the heavens. Today, according to Warren Weaver, the mathematical astronomer is asked at Cape Kennedy:

At precisely what speed, at precisely what angle, must a great
rocket be fired, and precisely how much must its trajectory be
altered, so that it can cruise out into space, and days or months
later, intersect the path of the Moon or Mars? This requires extensions and refinements of which Kepler and Newton never dreamed,
and calculations which would be wholly impossible were it not for
electronic computers.[1]

Could Leonardo have come to understand this tremendous
sequence? Could Ptolemy, or Euclid, or Aristotle? Their
brains were certainly good enough, but they would have
needed intensive exercise in disciplines then unborn, to say
nothing of the unavailability of electronic computers.

Dr. Weaver gives us a hint of what the scientific method has

[1] Pamphlet published by the Sloan Foundation in 1965.

already done for the mind. What it can do for the body, and for the community, is almost as miraculous—but with tragic overtones. It has revolutionized the human condition, in the sense of enormously increasing the span between birth and death, and of providing goods and services which in all former ages were beyond the reach, or even the imagination, of emperors and kings. In thermonuclear chain reactions, however, technology has posed a bleak alternative. Many writers have stated it, none perhaps more eloquently than the *New York Times* in an editorial: "whether the world becomes a near-paradise, or a radioactive hulk desolate in space."

WHAT IS TECHNOLOGY?

There are three major steps in this unique rational process.

First, some genius makes an important theoretical discovery in the field of energy, matter, evolution, genetics, behavior. After testing and formulating it, he announces a new scientific "law," and others eventually come to accept it. This process is usually regarded as "pure science" or pure research. Thorstein Veblen once labeled the motivation "idle curiosity."

Second, somebody else, with a more practical motivation, puts the new knowledge to work. He invents, say, a steam engine from the laws of thermodynamics, an atomic bomb from $E = mc^2$. This is the area of applied science, or *technology*—the domain of engineers and entrepreneurs, the step beyond pure science. The line between the two is not always sharp. In the Manhattan Project, for instance, new knowledge had to be found for the creation of plutonium, an element unknown in nature. Mostly, however, the Project was in the area of technology. Its goal was to take accredited scientific information about the atom, information developed by dozens of scientists over the past generation, and construct a workable bomb.

Third, the new invention enters the culture, to affect human behavior. Pure science as such has little impact on people, so long as it remains on the blackboard. Even primary inventions and constructs of applied science rarely have an immediate effect. Only when the invention or process is adopted by the Defense Department, or by a great industry, or is patented, advertised, and sold, does society at large begin to feel the effects. A powerful invention such as Watt's steam engine, or Faraday's electric motor, working over decades, changes behavior and culture patterns drastically around the world.

The distinction between pure and applied science appears in the modern symbol "R & D," where R stands for research in pure theory and D stands for the development of some practical application, for technology. We shall use R & D in this sense frequently in the pages to come.

Kenneth Boulding has made a simple and useful classification of knowledge about the world outside our heads.[2] First comes *folk knowledge* for the ordinary business of living—family, friends, the fields, the household, the village, the weather, and the market. This was the only kind of knowledge mankind possessed up to 5,000 years ago, and is still in constant and necessary use.

Then came *literary knowledge,* beginning with the account books of Sumeria, about 3000 B.C. It is knowledge written down and preserved—first practical records, then history, poetry, drama, the *Odyssey,* Herodotus, Aristotle, Shakespeare, Dante, Goethe. It is often inspiring, but not always an accurate description of the world outside. It contains the treasure trove of the humanities.

Galileo initiated *modern science,* the final step so far. "From the sixteenth century," says Boulding, "we find a small, but growing group of people who specialize in the increase of knowledge by a method which involves constant revision of images of the world under the impact of refined observation."

The climax of these observations to date, supported by in-

[2] *The Impact of the Social Sciences,* Rutgers University Press, 1966.

struments of almost diabolical refinement, is the journey of
astronauts around the planet, and, what is more, their safe
return to earth. Here is exact, dependable, repeatable knowledge about the cosmos; one decimal point missed and the
capsule may veer off and begin to orbit the sun, and so be lost
forever.

When technology becomes dynamic, people are forced to
change their accustomed ways. Farm boys leave the land for
the coal mines and the steel mills. Negroes, displaced by the
mechanical picker, leave the cotton fields, hoping for jobs in
the big cities. The shift may be resented and delayed in what
is called "cultural lag"—a fierce resistance against changing
old habits—or an invention may have almost immediate popular appeal, as in the case of electric light, television, and,
above all, the motorcar.

Years ago in Mexico I saw a corn grinder run by a Model T
Ford engine. It could do in a few minutes what a woman spent
six hours in doing with the traditional stone metate of the
Aztecs. When the grinder was first introduced in the village,
husbands protested and forbade its use: the tortillas, they said,
would not taste right. Their cultural lag was strong, but the
timeless principle of "least work," operating on the women,
was stronger. Six hours of hard labor, against five cheerful
minutes of watching a machine, made no sense. The corn
grinder was reintroduced, and this time it stuck. I often think
of this case, so clean-cut and so human, as a simple example of
how technology can aid people, and make human life more
comfortable and enjoyable. A contrary exhibit is to be found
in advertised "cures" for cancer. In most cases, however, a
new technical product carries both helpful and harmful effects,
with television as one outstanding example, and pesticides as
another.

"Technology" is therefore not an entity, a material thing in
space and time, which can be rounded up and photographed.
It is only a verbal label for the thousands of techniques and

inventions made possible by the advance of pure science. Each can affect the human condition for good or for ill or for both.

If modern science had not been inaugurated, if the best we had was literary knowledge, we would still be plowing with oxen, producing only handicraft goods, fighting small wars with muskets and cavalry charges, and treating the sick with leeches. The population of the world would be less than a quarter of what it is today, with a death rate of 40 per 1,000, and a growth rate probably below one percent a year. The fastest a man could travel would be 30 miles an hour on a horse.

THE SCIENTIFIC METHOD

There were plenty of superlative craftsmen and remarkable techniques before Galileo. Yet there existed no discipline or method for testing and preserving what was true and discarding what was false. A technique such as the manufacture of Damascus steel could be lost, while alchemy, astrology, and sheer magic survived to confuse the thinking of both philosophers and craftsmen. Thus Aristotle's conviction that the planets must move in perfect circles, since the circle was the most perfect curve, remained in vogue. The logic was complete: no further evidence was necessary.

Galileo used his mind differently. He was unimpressed with the logic of perfect circles, and called for observations and measurements which would show how the planets in fact did move—measurements upon which careful observers could agree. This kind of thinking—which met with strong resistance, even burnings at the stake—transformed astrology into astronomy, and alchemy into chemistry, and banished magic from the minds of educated men.

Bertrand Russell once observed that the essence of the scientific attitude is not to regard personal interests and desires as the key for understanding the world. Our inner feelings about perfect circles give way to controlled experiments. Percy Bridgman, in *The Logic of Modern Physics,* puts it dramatically: "The *fact* has always been for the physicist the one ultimate thing from which there is no appeal, and in the face of which the only possible attitude is a humility almost religious."

Few physicists welcomed the concept of relativity when it was introduced as an hypothesis by Einstein, early in the present century. But when the facts came in confirming it—as in the bending of light rays during an eclipse of the sun—they swallowed their personal feelings and accepted this modification of the majestic principles of Newton. (Physicists had come to develop almost a perfect-circle complex about Newton.)

It was hard, too, for some ingenious fellows to give up the hope of inventing a perpetual-motion machine. Even Leonardo worked on a wheel to turn itself forever by quicksilver. When the first and second laws of thermodynamics were established, however, all schemes for *perpetuum mobile* were outlawed. The Paris Academy of Science closed the door in 1775.

Here is a modern case involving the recent discovery of RNA, the chemical which appears to direct the development of an organism. Certain laboratory experiments indicated that a learned habit could be transferred from a trained rat to an untrained one by injecting brain RNA from the trained animal into the abdominal cavity of the untrained one. What a vista this would open up—if true! An animal need not bother to learn his tricks, just receive an injection. Was the conclusion accepted by other scientists? Professor Stephan L. Chorover of MIT reports in the *Technology Review* for December, 1966:

Together with investigators from more than half a dozen laboratories who independently set out to confirm the transfer of training by injection, we have failed to reproduce the reported results. Already there appear to have been more than 30 independent failures of this sort. The claimed transfer of training via injection thus remains an elusive phenomenon. Further work will be needed to explain why this is so.

The last sentence is critical. Professor Chorover does not call the original investigation a fraud; he does not even say the conclusion is wrong. He says he is unable to repeat it; 30 new experiments have not confirmed it. But even this is not conclusive: "Further work will be needed to explain why this is so." Here is the scientific method in its patient refusal to jump to conclusions, and in all its steadfast integrity.

THE HOW AND THE WHY

Water, as everyone knows, runs downhill. But it will run uphill too, in a siphon. Primitive engineers made it run so, but they did not know why it happened. Scientists after Galileo discovered why: the weight of air pressing down on the earth will force water up 32 feet, into a vacuum at sea level. Here we have a simple illustration of the stages in reaching a scientific law. First comes observation which can be checked by other observers, and is sharp enough to establish prediction. If you do *this,* then *that* will happen. If one arranges a siphon out of garden hose, he can suck water out of his cellar, through a high window, and away downhill. This is the *how* stage. The *why* stage, which is far more sophisticated, represents the true glory of science.

A good deal of natural science, and more social science, still stops at the "how" level, at simple prediction. The understanding level, finding why, is far advanced in physics, but has made only a modest start in studies of human behavior.

SCIENCE AND ETHICS

There is an impression among those with limited education that a scientist is a kind of cold, calculating machine, devoid of ethics and humanity. If ethics is defined as devotion to truth, nothing could be more false, as we noted in the training-by-injection experiments. The scientific method is one of systematic doubt; it carries with ease and confidence the idea: "This is an exciting hypothesis, but despite all my hard work, it can be wrong." In an earlier book, I tried to summarize the relationship of ethics to science in a paragraph which perhaps bears repeating:

Alone among man's activities, science can resolve problems independently of our desires and wills. . . . [The point made by Bertrand Russell.] To fudge an experiment, to slant a conclusion, to report anything but the whole truth as one knows it, alone in the night, brings ignominy and oblivion. There can be no secret processes, no patent medicines, no private understandings or payoffs on the side. The calculations must be laid on the table, face up, for all the world to see. In this sense, science is perhaps the most moral of all man's disciplines. It will be corrupted and debased if ever its direction falls permanently into the hands of national governments and ideologists. It is as international as the north wind.[8]

The scandal caused by Lysenko's interpretation of genetics in service to Russian propaganda under Stalin is an illustration of such corruption. The so-called "Pugwash Conferences" of scientists, from both sides of the Iron Curtain, where the good and evil effects of nuclear energy on human beings are honestly discussed, and joint recommendations made, illustrate the reverse, the profoundly ethical aspect of modern science.

At the 1967 annual meeting of the American Association for the Advancement of Science, the question of the responsi-

[8] *The Proper Study of Mankind*, Harper & Row, 1956.

bility of scientists was brought up. Their role in weather modification, in air and water pollution, pest control through such chemicals as DDT, and even R & D into racial differences was seriously discussed. One school of thought held that scientists should avoid investigating differences between the races;[4] another school held that inquiry should go forward, and that researchers have the obligation to denounce erroneous interpretations. T. Dobzhansky, the renowned geneticist, supported the latter school. He told the Association: "In our world a scientist has no right to be irresponsible." The distinguished audience applauded him.

J. Bronowski speaks of the "habit of truth" among scientists. When two of them discuss a scientific subject, they take it for granted that both are telling the truth. If this assumption did not hold, he says, "the entire scientific enterprise would collapse." When two politicians, or two businessmen, talk together, do they always believe each other?

EXPONENTIAL CURVE

Dr. Neal E. Miller of Yale agrees that man's brain has not changed in the last 50,000 years; but look, he says at these cultural changes:

Agriculture developed	10,000 years ago
The wheel invented	5,000 years ago
The steam engine	200 years ago
The airplane	60 years ago
Atomic energy utilized	20 years ago
Space vehicles (Sputnik)	10 years ago[5]

Compare the glacially slow progress of the early years with the torrent of knowledge flowing in during one's own lifetime—no part of it due to a change in the human brain, and every bit of it due to "the cumulative heritage of culture."

[4] Anthropologists, of course, have been analyzing racial differences for many years.

[5] See Oppenheimer *et al., The Scientific Endeavor,* in Reading List, p. 233.

Science and technology are said to be growing at an exponential rate, and Dr. Miller's timetable bears this out. Exponential means a growth rate like compound interest, a curve which becomes steeper over time. Professor Ritchie Calder notes in the *Bulletin of the Atomic Scientists* that the interval between the acquisition of new knowledge and assembly line production is growing shorter. "Before 1930," he said in 1965, "the median lapse was 33 years between the date of conception and the date of commercial success." But in the 1940's only four years and five months elapsed between $E = mc^2$ on the blackboard and the destruction of Hiroshima. The lone inventor of the past has become the research group of today. "The technologist translates the laboratory findings to the factory floor." Or to the surface of the moon.

Pure research on macromolecules leads to nylon. Research in solid-state physics leads to transistors. Industrial production of such items affords a profit, and the resulting economic affluence provides more money for research and so more affluence. A spiral up and up, as a recent editorial in *Science* explains:

The human brain has not changed significantly since the Ice Ages, but its products, growing exponentially, have violently affected the human condition. Scientific knowledge is doubling roughly every ten years. . . . This rapid advance is not only continually reordering the known facts of physical reality, but giving birth to new problems—such as the threat of automation, the danger of automobile exhaust pollutants. . . . The college educated citizen of today, aged 40, scarcely heard of, or imagined, during his years at school, any of the scientific-social problems he faces as an adult.

One might add that he had never heard of "set theory" in mathematics, a discipline with which his children now confound him on their return from school. Someone has calculated that half of all the scientists who ever lived are at work today. Someone else has calculated that an engineering graduate now has a "half-life" of only ten years, meaning that half of what he learned in school has then become obsolete, and half of what remains will be obsolete in another ten years.

FROM LOG CANOE TO THE *Queen Mary*

The late William F. Ogburn, professor of sociology at the University of Chicago, dramatically documented the growth of technology and its effect on people.[6] Only about 100 human generations have elapsed, he said, between the building of primitive canoes, hollowed out of logs, and the superliner *Queen Mary*. Evolution of the brain could not possibly account for this striking advance. The culture concept, however, can readily account for it. Techniques for building boats were handed down from father to son, improving gradually at first, and then suddenly, until enough knowledge had accumulated to build the great liner.

Ogburn charted Darmstaedter's monumental history of inventions. He charted the number of British patents and American patents, issued year by year. He charted major discoveries in physics, chemistry, geology, genetics, and medicine. All showed the familiar exponential curve. As a sociologist, he went on to list new social habits resulting from various inventions. The automobile, for instance, has revolutionized courting customs; radio has brought regions hitherto isolated into contact with world events.

A scientist like Alexander Humboldt could, in 1800, grasp the whole range of scientific knowledge, but no human mind is capable of grasping more than a small fraction of it today. Specialists in one discipline, say biology, are losing touch not only with other disciplines, but even with the latest findings in branches of their own specialty. More than half a million scientific papers appear every year, and librarians are quietly going mad trying to record them. This avalanche has been

[6] See Reading List.

aesthetic "illth"

called the "information explosion," and, as in the case of population, a reckoning cannot indefinitely be postponed.

With all this great storehouse of knowledge and its practical application, how much of it does one personally possess? Suppose the reader were cast away on an alien shore with only a box of tools. How long would it take him to design and build, say, a wheelbarrow?

ILLTH AND WEALTH

A good deal of the accumulated technology results in economic waste, some of it lethal and some just silly. Ruskin once termed this output "illth"—the opposite of wealth. Look around any supermarket, any drugstore, any automobile graveyard. Listen to almost any television program in the popular hours. Sample the ads in almost any newspaper. For example, a full-page advertisement in the *New York Times* in 1966, when fashion decreed very short skirts, shows a young lady, mostly legs, with the caption:

This is the way legs should look right now—buffed to a silken finish with "Secret Cover," Miss Arden's liquid leg makeup, with its own lamb's wool buffer. It stays on and on. In six pale-to-suntan shades. A rosy prospect for knees and heels.

Headlines opposite this alluring prose dealt grimly with the War on Poverty.

Illth has called forth many protests from philosophers and humanists, and indeed from many scientists who are appalled at the degradation of their primary output in pure research. I have even thrown a brick or two myself. But is it possible to imagine the Congress at Washington passing a law to forbid new invention, or to close up the Patent Office? We shall have to ride this curve out, taking the illth with the wealth for a long time to come.

The best we can hope for is to steer the flow by various

kinds of social and economic planning. Especially useful would be a panel of experts to canvass the effects on people, and on living space, before inventions are put into mass production.[7] As I write, Congress is belatedly wrestling with a law to build more safety into the design of motor cars, and so reduce the terrible slaughter on the roads.

This kind of planning has been well called "intelligent co-operation with the inevitable." Instead of trying to stop a major trend in full career, the planner seeks to deflect it into safer channels. Fortunately there are certain natural limits to exponential growth which can come to his aid. The curve of the "inevitable" sometimes flattens out and turns downward in the well-known "S-curve" of the engineer, which occurs when growth collides with some natural or biological barrier.

We will examine this important phenomenon in the next chapter, together with two all-out challenges to technology as such.

---

[7] We will expand this recommendation in the last chapter.

★

2

THE LIMITS OF TECHNOLOGY

TECHNOLOGY has brought us knowledge of both good and evil. Which will predominate? There are ardent pessimists as well as optimists. Many philosophers and indeed a few scientists see evil overcoming good. Jacques Ellul, philosopher and theologian, and Max Born, the world-renowned physicist, are both outstanding pessimists. In the development of science and technology, they say, man has taken the wrong road.

TWO CAVEATS

Ellul's denunciation is the more emphatic. He traces technics back to the Stone Age, and apparently distrusts everything from the first fist ax to the latest accelerator. Even rules for playing chess, he says, are a technic, hence deplorable. He fears that a dictatorship of technocrats is on the trend curve, and will be worse than Hitler's: "That it is to be a dictatorship of test tubes rather than hobnailed boots will not make it any less a dictatorship."

Why does Ellul in his book, *The Technological Society*,[1] weaken his case by extrapolating his denunciation to include practically all technical invention? Is it because he is an Aristotelian, and feels obliged to be totally consistent? We

[1] See Reading List.

15

can, of course, agree with him that much of applied science is inimical to the human condition, but not all of it.

Max Born, who, with Fritz Haber, introduced solid-state physics to the world, is also dismayed, though his argument seems less dogmatic. Technology or applied science, he says, contradicting Ellul, does not really go back to the Stone Age, it began with Galileo. The founder of modern science replaced crude trial and error, as well as proof based on verbal logic (perfect-circle thinking), with controlled experiments and careful measurements. From this revolutionary foundation, technology emerged "to change the world beyond recognition."

In his autobiography,[2] Born tells how he had led a happy and productive life in pure science, and also bridged the gap between the now familiar "two cultures," the humanities as contrasted with the sciences. Like his friends Einstein, Planck, and Heisenberg, he was a competent musician, and read deeply in Tolstoy, Kant, and Goethe. But when his generous, wide-ranging mind came up against the destruction of Hiroshima, suddenly his life's work seemed to fall in ashes around him. Here, in this stricken city, was the end of the road. He wrote, "The attempt made by nature on this earth to produce a thinking animal has failed."

Emphasizing the exponential growth of technology, Born notes other effects besides nuclear weapons. The internal combustion engine, he says, is putting unbearable strains on modern cities, while the bulldozer is destroying the surrounding countryside and the balance of nature. Automation, he feels, has degraded human work and undermined its dignity. His pessimism reaches its climax when he cries out:

I am haunted by the idea that this break in human civilization, caused by the discovery of the scientific method, may be irrepara-

[2] Published in the *Bulletin of the Atomic Scientists*, September—November, 1965.

ble. Though I love science, I have the feeling that it is so much against history and tradition that it cannot be absorbed. . . . Should the race not be extinguished by a nuclear war it will degenerate into a flock of stupid creatures under the tyranny of dictators who rule them with the help of electronic computers.

Thus Max Born joins Jacques Ellul in anticipating the defeat of Homo sapiens. They both expect computerized dictatorships, and both, one suspects, have been influenced by such prophetic pictures as Huxley's *Brave New World*, Orwell's *1984*, and "The Machine Stops" by E. M. Forster.[3] None of these seems able to discover an adequate ethical basis in science. Born, however, retains enough of the scientific attitude to conclude: "I may be wrong. . . . This is not a prophecy, just a nightmare."

BUT REGARD THE S-CURVE

No thoughtful person can brush aside the challenge. Pure science produced technology, technology produced thermonuclear weapons, and these can produce "a radioactive hulk, desolate in space." We must admit the distinct possibility of evil overcoming good in the broad sense of threatening human survival. There can be no quarrel with Born and Ellul on this point.

They seem to assume, however, together with many other pessimists, that technology in its various branches will go right on accelerating. There is something peculiarly alluring about a trend curve; one can hardly resist the temptation to prolong it indefinitely. If the price of food and clothing begins to rise, many of us will predict a ruinous inflation. If we note aggressive acts by China in South East Asia, we predict that nations will fall like dominoes, right up to Honolulu if not the Golden

[3] In *The Eternal Moment and Other Stories*, Harcourt, Brace, 1928. Reprinted in the Cornelius symposium, *Cultures in Conflict*. See Reading List.

Gate. Technology, too, we fear, will expand until the final Doomsday.

But suppose this does not happen; suppose another force intervenes to deflect the curve? Such forces already operate in many fields of both physics and biology, and these forces go far to counter the pessimism of Born and Ellul. This principle certainly deserves objective inquiry.

A clear and convincing case can be found in a recent book by John R. Platt, professor of biophysics, now at the University of Michigan.[4] Dr. Platt says that we look at the trends of technology in too brief a time scale. In our concentration we picture them as expanding indefinitely at the current rate. Look further, he says, and many trends, now ominous, will slow down. They will reach implacable limits, and presently become more stable states. A colony of bacteria grows exponentially until its nutrients run out.[5] The exponential growth curve bends over, flattens, and turns downward in the more general "S-curve," or logistic curve of growth. Like this:

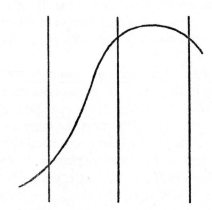

[4] *The Step to Man.* See Reading List.
[5] A garbage dump near Boston which supported between 4,000 and 6,000 herring gulls lost all but 100 of them within two weeks after a large incinerator was built, according to Charlton Ogburn in his book, *The Winter Beach.*

There are physical, not to say economic and social, limits to a good deal of technological advance, says Dr. Platt, and we are already on the threshold of a number of steady-state conditions. Contrary to popular belief, we are not, he insists, at the beginning of continuous acceleration, but in the middle of a transitional crisis, one altogether unique in human history. The slowing-down phase is already in operation, and will grow clearer in the period immediately ahead. The year 2000, subject to a series of S-curves, promises to look very different than it would if all trends continued at current rates. Dr. Platt is not saying that growth will stop entirely, but that the *rate* of growth will level off, which is a very different proposition. He is saying that physical conditions governing growth will change, and force the rate of growth downward.

Take, he says, the speed of *communication*. When we are able to transmit sight and sound around the world in two seconds, as is now possible, no acceleration in speed can affect television and radio. A limit has been reached.

Take *transport*. The steam locomotive surpassed the speed of the fastest bird a century ago, at 70 miles an hour. Jet liners now travel at 600 mph, while supersonics have flown experimentally at 2,000 mph, and rocket planes at 4,000 mph are on the drawing board. Draft this trend over the past 100 years, and you have a truly exhilarating exponential curve! How long can it continue? Even if faster transport can be developed, what earthly use would it have on this small planet? We can now send men to any point on the globe in less than a day. Will six hours by supersonic plane—with its devastating sonic boom—or one hour by rocket plane make a difference which is worth the fabulous extra cost in money, noise, and nervous tension?

Take *bombs*. The 20-ton blockbuster of World War II accelerated first to the 20,000-ton Hiroshima bomb, and now to Russia's 60-million-ton thermonuclear terror. A 100-million-ton bomb, or even larger, could be built, but it would have no useful purpose beyond political threatening. The practical limit has been reached, and indeed overreached.

Take *population*. Dr. Platt is not the only scientist who sees an S-curve coming here. At present rates of growth there will be close to seven billion people on earth by the year 2000, and 25 billion long before the end of the following century—eight times the present population. Try to picture eight times as many cars on the road, eight times as many people in the supermarkets and the subways, eight times as many on the public beaches. Such a growth is hardly conceivable. As in the case of herring gulls, plagues of locusts, and herds of deer, growth rates must plunge downward when the nutrients or the resources run out.

For the long run, population increase is the most important problem facing mankind; growth must slow down drastically in the next few years. But will the change be orderly or chaotic? We will examine this question at more length in the next two chapters.

Dr. Platt presents case after case where the S-curve is beginning to replace acceleration. Pure science, however, in the sense of accredited knowledge, can go on expanding indefinitely,[6] provided it stays on the blackboard out of the hands of technologists and engineers. This provision is, however, improbable. Sooner or later, useful knowledge has always been put to work, as Heisenberg said in 1934:

> The task of pure science is to clear and prepare the ground for the growth of technical development. . . . A neglect of pure science would be a symptom of the exhaustion of the forces which condition both technical progress and science.[7]

Once we grasp their significance, we can see S-curves forming in areas not mentioned by Dr. Platt. Take internal com-

[6] "Pure science," according to C. P. Snow, "is the search for the unknown . . . it will linger on inexorably."
[7] *Naturwissenschaften*, Vol. 40.

bustion engines—the complex of automobiles, trucks, buses, tractors, and bulldozers, to say nothing of outboard motors. How many outboards, towing skiers, can a square mile of water tolerate? Water policemen are already beginning to appear: Long Island Sound on a bright summer weekend is on the verge of chaos.

More seriously, how long can cars and trucks and buses continue to poison the air before the limit of human tolerance is reached? Los Angeles and New York seem already on the verge, as we shall see later.

THE LOVED ONE

No branch of technology in recent years has so affected human living as the motorcar—not only in the United States, but increasingly throughout the world. It has bestowed large benefits upon the people of high-energy societies, and, until recently, the net effect seemed to be heavily on the asset side. But now the liabilities are coming in, in the form not only of polluted air, but of monstrous traffic jams, parking problems, the disruption of family life due to extreme mobility, slaughter on the highways, the getaway car of criminals, the blacktop wasteland.

No institution in America is permitted to stand in the way of the motorcar. No local government yet dares bar it from the city. Let it strangle the downtown area, scatter supermarkets, subdivisions, and junk heaps over the countryside, kill and maim and poison—all is forgiven the loved one. It not only warms the heart, glittering in its chromium out there at the curb; it confers prestige and status, it thrills the senses like a roller coaster. Perhaps most important of all, the motorcar symbolizes freedom and escape. Step on the accelerator and away we go, away from it all, away from our troubles and responsibilities. . . . True, the freedom has almost gone in city traffic, but the dream remains. The *New York Times* describes a Ferrari car:

The steering is sharp and very accurate, the equivalent of a hair trigger on a gun. The acceleration comes up through the gears smoothly, and very, very fast, and always there is the feeling of extra power, extra speed—in a machine like this nothing can stop a man, nothing can catch him, nothing resist him. He is emperor and daredevil at one and the same time. . . .

The cult is accelerating everywhere. An official of the Russian Gosplan told me in Moscow that the popular demand for motorcars was massive, but that the state would not manufacture them in volume until the planners could provide a place to park them. Detroit has no such scruples. Dearly as we love our cars, however, the S-curve cannot be many years away.[8] The limits of tolerance in big cities and their suburbs, limits which are both physical and chemical, are being reached.

At the end of 1966, according to the Automobile Manufacturers' Association, there were 94 million cars, trucks, and buses on U.S. roads—one for every two persons in the nation. They burned 75 billion gallons of gas and diesel fuel during the year. Four out of five families drove a car, one family out of five drove two cars or more, and 40 million women had a driver's license. How long can this curve go on mounting?

BIOLOGICAL LIMITATIONS

Powerful support for the S-curve thesis comes from Dr. René Dubos of the Rockefeller Institute. He pointed out in a recent paper at Santa Barbara that mankind acquired its genetic code (DNA) during the late Paleolithic period, and has not changed significantly since that time. "From the bio-

---

[8] A woman in England, says the London *Times,* so loved her Austin that when it expired she had it crushed into a column of metal, first as an ornament in her garden, then to become the headstone for her grave.

logical point of view, modern man is indeed almost identical with ancient man." Does this not mean that a healthy baby, born to a Cro-Magnon woman say 30,000 years ago, transported magically to a kindly family in Middletown, Ohio, would grow up little different from other children in the block? And vice versa? Presently we shall meet the American Indian Ishi, who, after living some 50 years in the Stone Age, moved smoothly forward 10,000 years into the twentieth century.

The unchangeability of man's genes, says Dr. Dubos, defines certain limits beyond which technology cannot force him. We are constrained by the frontiers of man as much as by the frontiers of technology. Unfortunately, he says, we know more about technology than we do about man. Here, of course, is the frontier of social science and its great importance in a time of rapid change.

Some interesting laboratory work concerned with the limits of human performance is now going on. What does weightlessness do to an astronaut's performance? How many dials can an airplane pilot watch efficiently? A man, the scientists say, takes *inputs* from his senses—eye, ear, nose—then transforms these signals in his "central processor" or brain, into *outputs,* or instructions to his motor system. You see a dog ahead of you on the road (input), and down comes your foot on the brake (output).

It is now pretty well verified that a man can attend to only one input at a time. To do more overloads his central processor, and no appropriate action may result. If, at the instant you see the dog, you hear a sharp explosion off to the left, you cannot react to both signals simultaneously. John W. Senders, in *Science and Technology,* makes this significant statement:

Man is not a machine like a computer. His performance is limited by his physical structure, his physiology, his psychology.

. . . The need to understand the limits of human performance is something that has crept up on us in the last few decades without our being aware of it. We have become involved in manned space flight, seen the advent of 200-passenger commercial aircraft, and watched without apparent concern as the highways have filled with high-speed machines operated by indifferently trained drivers. All of this has occurred without any real understanding of how much demand these tasks place on humans.[9]

Can speeds and timing be increased indefinitely? Of course they cannot; the central processor will become overloaded.

How much technology can a man take? He can take a lot, for he is the most adaptable of earth's creatures. The pool of human genes will permit a man to adapt to the Sahara, the Antarctic, Harlem, Mount Everest, or a space capsule in orbit —at least for a time. Human cultures are diverse, but not completely; all cultures share a number of universals, such as a structured language. At some point our genetic equipment will cry out "Stop!" It may be that both *Brave New World* and *1984* are beyond the limit. Certainly some of the predicted horrors of the technological future are out of bounds; S-curves will move in to prevent them.

THE CASE OF ISHI

Human adaptability is strikingly illustrated in the unique story of Ishi, the last American who lived in a complete Stone Age culture.[10] Ishi came out of the wild country around Mount Lassen in California in 1911, the sole survivor of his tribe, and gave himself up to the white man lest he die of starvation. The local sheriff promptly threw him into jail, from which he was rescued by a distinguished anthropologist, Alfred Kroeber, who realized what a priceless find had been made.

[9] July, 1966.
[10] As narrated by Theodora Kroeber. See Reading List.

Could a wild man from the hills adjust to modern civilization? He could and did. Ishi—a term meaning "man" in his native tongue—lived for some years in the technological culture of the twentieth century before he died, at probably close to 60 years of age.

Ishi learned enough English to tell Dr. Kroeber about the tragic end of his people, and to describe the nomadic hunting culture which they followed. He stayed at the University Museum of Anthropology in San Francisco, worked there, and demonstrated the artifacts of his tribe, while he observed with a shrewd eye the artifacts, behavior, and follies of the urban culture around him. He was gentle, affectionate, very clean in his personal habits, curious, and a superb craftsman.

He came to admire the houses of civilization, which protected one from cold and damp much better than a cave. Running water, from faucets and flush toilets, he found marvelous. So were electric lights, gas stoves, and the telephone. He wore with pride a watch which was given him, keeping it wound, but not set; he told time by some private system of his own. Automobiles interested him, but not to compare with trolley cars, and the delightful "woosh" of their air brakes. He was on the flying field when Harry Fowler took off for one of the first cross-continental flights. Ishi did not share the excitement of the crowd; he found the plane a poor thing compared to an eagle.

He was highly selective about the tools put at his disposal. Hatchet, saw, knife, hammer—yes; auger, chisel, plane—no. He rarely used level or square, and instead of a ruler preferred to measure by spread of palm, or by fingertip to elbow. But he found a small bench vise far better than his big toe for holding a bow during its masterly construction.

After his harrowing initiation into the twentieth century via the police department, it did not take Ishi long to come to terms with the new environment—a jump of perhaps 10,000 years. He selected those artifacts and customs which pleased him, helped him in his work, and made him more comfortable. Food apparently was no problem. Once, with Dr. Kroeber, he returned to the Mount Lassen country, where he acted as an expert guide; but he had no desire to remain. He was a man of great goodwill so far as human beings were concerned, and he took many aspects of technology in stride.

One cannot read Mrs. Kroeber's delightful and well-documented account of Ishi without realizing again that "technology" cannot be packaged as an entity, either good or bad. The vast battery of new artifacts and customs that Ishi encountered on the whole amused and contented him. He made the adjustment. Are the rest of us doomed, as Professors Born and Ellul so stoutly affirm?

SUMMARY

"Technology" cannot be judged as a whole except in a very limited sense. But if Ishi, a man from the Stone Age, accepted the early twentieth century in San Francisco, cannot human beings born in the 1960's adjust to still more rapid change? Before attempting an answer, the careful observer must ask: What kind of change; what kind of technology, where and when? And who is exposed to it? We must try to assess the effect, good, bad, or neutral, on human beings, remembering that one branch—say, internal combustion engines—may have a whole spectrum of effects.

For the next generation we shall probably have to face a frightening multiplication of technologies. We must try to hold them within bounds of human toleration, supporting men like Dr. Senders in studying these limits more intensively than ever before. As the crises mount—population, automation, living space—they may call forth one major effort after another, in which the United States, and hopefully the world, can set aside political infighting and concentrate on a united policy for the race.

The crucial factor is *time*. Has the human race time enough to adjust to the various impacts, as Ishi adjusted? Dr. Platt believes that the test will not be prolonged more than two decades. He compares it to the shock front on the wing of a supersonic plane. We are at present, he says, on the edge of a pressure wave with abnormal turbulence. But if the shock front can be passed, a calmer period lies beyond, one where exponential change gives way to a steady-state condition.

We look beyond the current shock front to a wealthy and powerful and coordinated world society, reaching across the solar system; a society that might find out how to keep itself alive and evolving for thousands or millions of years. . . . It is a tremendous prospect. It is a quantum jump.

It is indeed. But our current study of the most probable world cannot begin with quite such a tremendous assumption —a full-fledged Utopia to counter the nightmare of Max Born. Dr. Platt goes on to insist that "the world is now too dangerous for anything less than Utopia"—an observation for both optimists and pessimists to work on.

Our brief excursion along the shock front, described in these two initial chapters, indicates that while technology has been expanding at an exponential rate since Galileo, various branches are running into physical and biological limits, where the S-curve takes over. There are, however, no limits to the pursuit of pure science.

Applied science has enormously increased the world's population to the point of becoming mankind's most serious problem. It has disrupted long-established cultural patterns, such as the family and the nation-state. It has made nuclear war an exercise in mutual suicide, and thus given impetus to the idea of one world. It has diminished the area fit for permanent habitation on this planet, but at the same time it gives promise of a material Utopia based on unlimited energy from nuclear power plants.

Finally, technology has helped to develop the scientific attitude, where one's personal desires are subordinated to what is true—true about the physical world and true about human behavior, including oneself.

3

MULTIPLYING PEOPLE

OF ALL the individual trends generated by technology, the increase in population at an exponential rate is rapidly becoming the most ominous, displacing even the arms race. Though the population of the world is not known to the decimal point, demographers are now able to estimate it within dependable limits. When Robert C. Cook of the Population Reference Bureau[1] in Washington was asked what was meant by the term "population explosion," he gave this graphic reply: "It means that world population is now doubling in 35 years. The last time it doubled took 80 years. The time before that took 200 years. That is the population explosion."

No expert is needed to see that world population, at this rate, will double again in some 15 years, and long before A.D. 2100 the phrase "standing room only" will have a good deal of cogency. On the other hand, it does not need a biological physicist like Dr. Platt to predict that long before any such notice is put up in the lobby of the world theater, the rate will slacken and begin to bend backward in an S-curve.

The population of the world as I write is estimated at 3.3

---

[1] Much of the data in this chapter come from this excellent Bureau and its monthly *Bulletin*; see Reading List. Other useful organizations continue to arise, including the Population Crisis Committee, the Hugh Moore Fund, the Planned Parenthood Federation, etc.

billion. If it doubles in 35 years it will be 6.6 billion by the end of the century. What causes such a rate of growth? There are two major causes, both due to technology.

After a relatively slow growth to the middle of the eighteenth century, population was stimulated by the industrial revolution, which greatly increased the output of goods, the standard of living, health, and fertility. It was also stimulated by the opening of new lands in the Western Hemisphere and Australia, which increased the world's food supply. Thus a vigorous growth in the number of people was largely the result of a vigorous growth in applied science—the steam engine, the steamship, the railroad, the moldboard plow. Failing these new techniques, persisting high birth rates would still have been matched by high death rates.

Early in this century came another technical advance, which expanded into what is now called the population explosion. It began with the conquest of yellow fever, by eliminating malaria mosquitoes during the building of the Panama Canal. Presently modern preventive medicine, employing inoculations, antibiotics, DDT, sanitation, sharply reduced the death rate, not only in affluent societies but all over the world. The birth rate continued at par, and through the widening gap population poured. The major effect of the new techniques was to reduce infant mortality, so that more girls grew to maturity to become mothers. Thus total population increased rapidly, with no increase in individual fertility; indeed, the number of children per family might even decline.

The world growth rate was estimated at 1.8 percent in 1955, at 2.1 percent ten years later in 1965, and is expected to reach 2.4 percent in 1975. At this rate population doubles in less than 30 years. Today in 1967, 8,000 babies are born somewhere in the world every hour, 70 million every year; by 1970 there will be 300 million more mouths to feed.[2] Said the

[2] Figures from the Hugh Moore Fund, New York.

White House Conference on International Cooperation in 1965: "The rate of growth of world population is so great, and its consequences so grave, that this may be the last generation to cope with the problem on the basis of free choice."

It is interesting to remember the strong warning raised during the earlier period of technological advance. The Reverend Thomas Malthus in 1798 wrote a famous essay, in which he pointed out that while food production tended to grow at an arithmetic rate (2, 4, 6, 8), population tended to grow at a geometric, or exponential, rate (2, 4, 8, 16). In due time, said Malthus, forecasting a population explosion, people will increase so much faster than their food that wholesale starvation must result. The statistics of that day, however, were inadequate to check the prediction, and Dr. Malthus's theory remained unconfirmed. Now, a century and a half later, Malthusianism is again receiving respectful attention. Population growth in relation to food supply is being recognized not only as a domestic problem in nearly every country, but as a global issue.

Beginning about 1960, estimates showed the amount of food available per person decreasing. This caused Director Binay Sen of the United Nation's Food and Agricultural Organization to say:

It is no less than seven years since there was any appreciable increase in food production per head of the world's population, seven very lean years. . . . In the Far East and in Latin America, per capita production is less than it was before the war. . . .

A SYMBOL AND A WARNING

The effect of modern medical technology is well illustrated by an analysis of what has happened to the island of Mauritius in the Indian Ocean.[3] In 1946 the population was 428,000 in an area about half the size of Long Island, New York. Many

[3] *Population Bulletin, August,* 1962.

---

people suffered from malaria and died of it. Then DDT arrived, together with other remedies for tropical diseases. What, one asks, could be more beneficent? In five years the death rate fell from 36 per thousand to 14, while the birth rate increased slightly. By 1961 population had grown by 50 percent, to 656,000, due almost entirely to an excess of births over deaths; there was no in-migration. Children under 15 increased much more rapidly than other age groups and life expectancy, of course, rose. If these rates continue, says the Reference Bureau, Mauritius will be swamped by two million persons by the year 2000, and "a pleasant island reduced to indescribable misery."

Mauritius is not only a symbol of the population explosion, but also a solemn warning of how the application of technology, even a variety which initially is most humane, can upset the balance of nature and develop into tragedy. The death rate goes down, the birth rate stays high, and as more and more people try to exist on the same resource base, living standards decline. This is the formula which now prevails in the developing nations of Asia, Africa, and Latin America. The term "Hungry World," coined by John Scott in his book *Democracy is Not Enough,* characterizes the area well, and I shall use it frequently.

THREE RATES OF GROWTH

The crisis in population affects the whole planet, and produces a variety of results. Hardship is of course more severe in poor countries like Mauritius, but rich countries are also affected, though in different ways, as we shall see. Nations can be classified into those with low, medium, or high growth rates, as follows:[4]

Group 1. Affluent countries with limited space, such as

[4] Following Nathan Keyfitz in the *Bulletin of the Atomic Scientists,* March, 1966.

those of Western Europe and Japan. Population here now totals about 500 million. The group is growing at *less* than one percent a year, and at this rate will double in a century or so. No serious explosion in this group . . . yet.

Group 2. Affluent countries with more ample space, including the U.S., Russia, Canada, Australia, Argentina. Population in this group also totals about 500 million. The group is growing at around 1.5 percent a year, and at this rate will quadruple in about a century. This is too fast for comfort in some areas, but the over-all situation is not seriously explosive . . . yet.

Group 3. The Hungry World—most of Asia, Africa, and Latin America. Population in this group is now estimated at two billion—double the total of groups 1 and 2. It is growing at close to 3 percent a year, twice group 2, four times group 1. At this rate there will be 16 billion human beings in the Hungry World in 100 years, eight times the present number, and more than five times the population of groups 1 and 2 combined.

In summary, the affluent societies will grow at present rates from 1 billion to 3, the nonaffluent from 2 billion to 16, the whole world from 3 billion to 19 on Dr. Keyfitz's calculations —which are not out of line with other projections. But of course any such expansion is both biologically and spatially impossible. Long before the end of another century, the S-curve will take over due to lack of food.

The real question is whether growth rates will fall primarily because of disaster or because of birth control. The amount of food which can be made available may delay the crisis by a few years but will not change the end result.

YEAR OF DECISION

Until very recently most people viewed the population explosion on a par with flying saucers—the result, they said, of overheated imagination if not overworked statistics. We can always grow more food, they said; look at the American food surplus. Look, they said, Americans were worried about slow growth and the bad effect on business in the late 1930's; that cycle will come back again. As for birth control, they said, do not publicize that unfortunate issue; it will only lead to more immorality.

The issue, however, would not down, and in the year 1965 a watershed seems to have been crossed. Quite suddenly the true outlines of the problem came into public focus. Reports from the United Nations and various U.S. Government departments, from President Johnson, from Sweden and other foreign nations, the phenomenal story of Japan's birth control campaign, the U.S. War on Poverty, even the appointment of a committee by the Pope in Rome—all combined in 1965 to put population and its control on the front pages. Presently everyone who could read a newspaper or listen to a serious program on the air knew that the situation was becoming ominous. Senator Ernest Gruening's committee on the Population Crisis went on accumulating impressive evidence from the highest sources.

THE MAN-LAND RATIO

Serious students also began to realize that the situation was none too good in all the affluent societies, especially the United States. They began to grasp the unpleasant fact that the population crisis will not be solved when the growth rates of poor countries are brought into line with those of the rich, for the affluent themselves are in a similar fix, only with a longer period of grace. If people continue to increase, while their living space remains the same, or, worse, declines, the time must come when the limits of viability are reached. It may take a decade, it may take a century, but it will come.

In the United States, the man-land ratio is changing even

faster than population growth alone would warrant. The more goods and gadgets a society demands—under the spur of high-pressure selling and planned obsolescence—the more goods and resources are needed to *offset* the wastes that attend afflu-ence—for example, pollution, erosion, water shortages, traffic jams, urban sprawl. Modern plumbing and sanitation, proudly hailed as American inventions, depend on ample supplies of pure water. The pure water is quickly used and discarded as impure water to pollute rivers and harbors. We shall see in Chapter 5 how various natural resources, some of them irre-placeable, are being consumed even more rapidly than people multiply.

Dr. Harrison Brown, Nobel laureate, provides us with a simple analogy. All life, he says in *The Challenge of Man's Future*,[5] goes back to the rate at which photosynthesis takes place. This determines the amount of plant life, which in turn determines animal life, including man. The interrelationships between living species are of course complex, and are studied in the science of ecology. To simplify the matter, says Dr. Brown, let us take just two species, grass and rabbits, and see what happens. The more grass is available, the healthier the rabbits, and the more baby rabbits are born. The more rabbits, however, the more rapidly grass is eaten up. Eventually an equilibrium must be reached, where both the amount of grass and the number of rabbits remain approximately constant.

Nature, which is said to abhor a vacuum, also abhors an unchecked growth rate, and will correct it violently if neces-sary. If a given human society demands modern medicine with its low death rate and long life span, *it must limit its birth rate*. There is no way out of this mathematical and biological vise.

There is a simple equation which, like grass and rabbits, also illustrates the situation. If L stands for the average stan-

[5] See Reading List.

dard of living, and O stands for the output of goods, including food, and P stands for population, then:

$$L = \frac{O}{P}$$

Living standards are roughly determined by production divided by population. Accordingly, living standards cannot rise unless production increases *faster* than population. In the Hungry World the current record shows the reverse—population increasing faster than output. It follows that average standards of living must go down.

During the years 1960 to 1965, for example, the production of food in Latin America increased by 6 percent, but population increased by 11 percent. Applying these figures to the equation, we see that the standard of living in Latin America as a whole has gone down. During the same period in Western Europe, the reverse was true: food production went up 11 percent, population only 4 percent. Fitting this into the equation, living standards should show a gain—which they did.

We are thus forced to agree with the American Academy of Sciences when it says: "There can be no doubt concerning the long term prognosis: Either the birth rate of the world must come down or the death rate must go back up."

In any given community, where a planning board is trying to plan for optimum density, four variables must be dealt with: the birth rate, the death rate, the rate of in-migration, the rate of out-migration. California, for example, must deal with all of them. For the whole world, however, the migrations cancel out—unless and until we begin to populate the solar system. *Deaths must balance births, so that the growth rate is around zero, if the planet is to be permanently viable.*[6]

---

[6] This flat conclusion is very forcibly argued by George Macinko in *Science*, July 30, 1965.

At what total? It has not yet been calculated, but I would guess that it could hardly exceed 10 billion persons—a far cry from standing room only—and would be a good deal more manageable and comfortable with five billion, which will be reached in 1985 or so.

PROBLEMS OF AFFLUENT SOCIETIES

Every country in the world is threatened by the population explosion, but at different dates. The affluent one-third of mankind has various special population problems. We will devote the rest of this chapter to some of these. In the next chapter we will try to assess special problems of the Hungry World.

A low-energy society gives way to one of high energy when one crosses the Rio Grande going north. (Whether people are any happier to the north is of course debatable—what does one mean by happiness?) Per capita income increases some tenfold, the literacy rate rises above 90 percent—despite a scandalously large army of North American nonreaders. The production of food is so much greater than citizens can eat that Washington has been paying out billions of dollars over the years to keep food crops off the market.

But rapid growth raises severe problems other than food. They include old people, the baby boom in the United States, the problems of people unemployed, maladjusted, and settling in the wrong place.

WE ARE LIVING LONGER

Sometimes it helps understanding to push a trend to its extreme logical limits. If nobody ever died, the growth rate would equal the birth rate, and strange things would begin to happen. First of all we would see a relative increase in young children, but presently an alarming increase in people over 65, an increase which would keep on expanding. People in the middle years would have to work harder and harder to support overhead costs at both ends of the scale. Medicare projects would presently go bankrupt.

Fortunately in the real world, people will go on dying, but as technology pushes the death rate down, life expectancy automatically goes up. It now stands at about 70 years in the United States, as against 40 years in India. This means more old people relatively, a massive trend which affects every society where death rates are falling, but affluent societies with particular vindictiveness. It is harder to be an old person in America now than it was in my grandfather's time.

This may seem a strange conclusion, but one has only to take a tour through some of our nursing homes to realize how true it is. A high-energy society steadily increases the relative number of elderly people, while it steadily undermines their position in the culture. In the old days they had more prestige and far more function. Says social scientist Irving Rosow:

> Old people's skills, experience and knowledge are no longer critical factors in our culture, and seldom make them authorities. The speed and pervasiveness of social change now transforms the world within a generation, so that the experience of the old becomes largely irrelevant to the young.

When I was a boy, in a time when a motorcar was a rarity, the iceman brought the 60-pound block to the kitchen door with a rubber pad on his back, I studied my homework by gaslight, and no man had ever flown; in most families that I knew, old people lived with their children. Now, if an American male, 65 or over, can maintain his health, his income, his work, and his marriage—four cardinal possessions—he has no great problem. How many of us are so fortunate? If he is poor, or ill, or retired, or a widower, the world has little place for him. This unprecedented situation is partly alleviated by old age pensions and Medicare programs. When the state pays the doctor, however, it does not improve the prestige of the

"The Death of M."

patient—rather the reverse. Julius Horwitz, an experienced investigator with the New York Department of Welfare, puts the case bluntly. The aged in a big city have no economic status, he says; they have no status in the household, they have no vocational skills to pass on to the younger generation. "Their special problem is survival in a society which finds their minds and bodies superfluous."

We are a long way from the traditional Council of Elders, which once dominated the tribe in peace and war. One has to accompany the anthropologists back to primitive societies to find it.

THE BABY BOOM

Turning from oldsters to youngsters, we note a special problem in the United States due to the boom in babies which followed World War II. During the Great Depression of the 1930's, the population growth rate—not the total population, of course—declined, and most demographers predicted a continuing decline. The war rudely upset these predictions. It brought full employment, high wages, and earlier marriages. Soon the growth rate was reversed and began to climb. The tidal wave of babies born in the late 1940's presently reached the labor market. By 1964, 400,000 more young people were looking for work than in 1960. At the same time automation was reducing the demand for unskilled and semiskilled workers. This distortion of the growth pattern was the primary reason for the great army of unemployed youngsters in the midst of American prosperity in the 1960's, and for some of the race riots in big cities. The distortion encourages the breakup of families, it encourages juvenile delinquency, vandalism, and traffic accidents. The postwar baby boom, according to Dr. Philip Hauser of the University of Chicago, is exacting a high price from the American people.

PEOPLE IN THE WRONG PLACE

Political scientist Harvey Wheeler of Santa Barbara outlines another serious U.S. population problem. It should not be too difficult, he says, in this big country to accommodate another 150 million people somewhere. But where? The real difficulty is density—plenty of wide-open spaces here, serious over-crowding there. People, he says, do not automatically go where they cause the least trouble, as in frontier days; they usually do the opposite. Today poor people are leaving the land and flooding into city slums, while the middle class is flooding out to the suburbs.

Take Los Angeles, says Wheeler. Every month enough new people move in to populate a sizable town. But they do not bring along their schools, roads, parking places, water supply, sewers, hospitals. Worse still—and this is a most important point—they leave their *cultural* system behind them too, and there isn't one for them to join when they arrive. Los Angeles must in effect equip a new town every month with all utilities, and find new jobs as well. It must also "make available the commodity it least possesses: a ready-made cultural system."

The uprising of Negroes in the slum district called Watts in 1965 is thus accounted for in part. The rioters came largely from rural areas in the South, and there was no place for them to fit into—no economic place, no cultural pattern. They felt hostility and prejudice among Los Angeles citizens, especially the police. All major U.S. cities, indeed many cities in affluent areas around the world, are confronted with this dilemma: too many people in the wrong place.

Not only Los Angeles but the whole state of California has a density problem.[7] It is now the most populous state in the Union, with 19 million people. Every day it grows by some

[7] *Population Bulletin,* June, 1966.

1,500 persons, the net result of births, deaths, people moving in and moving out. The state has a well-publicized image of paradise on earth, and so the determining variable is in-migration. At this rate California will have 25 million people by 1980, and 50 million by the end of the century—about the population of present-day France.

The state, of course, has everything—a marvelous Pacific Coast, snowcapped mountains, great redwood trees, rich soils, water power, fabulous oil fields. But only about 10 million acres are really suitable for living space, and bulldozers are tearing up 140,000 acres a year for housing developments. More serious are problems of air and water. The notorious smog of Los Angeles is now spreading to other urban areas, its prime cause automobile exhausts. Water is pumped from the Colorado River, 300 miles away, but air cannot be pumped in. San Francisco Bay is grossly polluted and so is lovely Lake Tahoe in the mountains.

In Asia, Africa, and Latin America, it is food which will eventually limit the growth of people, and famine is the force in nature that equalizes the birth rate and the death rate. What is now happening in California is equally ominous, but the "nutrients" are of a different order. Not famine, but the shrinkage of living space is the determining factor.

California, like Mauritius, is a symbol and a warning, but it is situated in a high-energy society, blessed with all the artifacts of prosperity. The air-conditioned house with its five bathrooms, the two air-conditioned cars in its garage, the heated swimming pool—how pleasant they are today in Beverly Hills. How long can they prevail against tomorrow?

Other effects already tend to bedevil the affluent. One is a plague of statistics. We are being automated and computerized at a frightening rate. Hardly anyone likes it, yet rapid growth demands it. The telephone company says that without automated service it could not possibly handle its present volume of business, and certainly government could not handle Social Security without computers. When there are 500 million Americans, shall we have lost our names entirely and depend for individual existence on a punch card and an index number?

Up to a few years ago, an increase in the population of an American community was regarded as good for business; Chambers of Commerce even tried to boost the Census figures. Today, as the costs of congestion mount, the story is different. "It is high time," said a speaker at the 1966 meeting of the National Industrial Conference Board, "that businessmen cease looking upon the stork as a bird of good omen."

It is manifest that a doubling of the world's population in a generation has monstrously distorted traditional patterns. It is manifest that technology is at the bottom of it, specifically modern medicine. All humanity is affected, with some special repercussions in high-energy societies, as we have seen.

Now let us turn to trends in low-energy countries below the Rio Grande, and in Asia and Africa, together with their problems of food, famine, and birth control.

☆

4

THE CONTROL OF POPULATION

PROFILE OF THE HUNGRY WORLD

Latin America, Asia, and Africa comprise the Hungry World, where, considering the area as a whole, population is now outrunning subsistence, and where the formula $L = \dfrac{O}{P}$ shows the standard of living going down. Dr. Roy E. Brown of the University of East Africa has drawn a profile of this vast area, setting forth its major characteristics. His vantage point for viewing it is of course unexcelled.

Its economy, he says in *Science*,[1] is based on subsistence agriculture; 90 percent of its people are rural.

The average per capita income is less than $200 a year.

Fewer than half the adults can read or write.

Technicians are short in all fields.

Birth rates are high, and despite a high rate of infant mortality, population for the whole area is growing at about 3 percent a year—a rate which doubles in 23 years.

Half the population is under 15 years old.

Unemployment in the villages is causing a mass movement to the cities, where unemployment is usually worse. (This corresponds to a similar trend in the U.S., as we have noted.)

[1] July 15, 1966.

Reforms are seriously handicapped by superstititions, taboos, fatalism, rigid diet customs—rice eaters, for instance, reject wheat.

The lower death rates achieved through preventive medicine add to the number of old, sick, and hungry people, and thus tend to make the population crisis more severe.

Finally, as Dr. Brown observes, the rich nations are giving the poor nations little effective help. The crisis has not yet been squarely faced by either group.

This brings up an interesting comparison. Karl Marx predicted that, under capitalism, the rich would grow richer and the poor poorer. He was of course talking about economic classes—and he was wrong. The rich in open societies are not gaining too much after the income tax gets through with them, while the sometime "masses" have risen from the lower brackets to the middle class, and become the driving force of the affluent society. Even the truly poor today—in the United States this means about 20 percent of families—have enough to eat, in bulk if not in vitamins. When it comes to nations, however, the Marxian prediction holds. While affluent societies grow richer, at least in gross national product, the Hungry World grows hungrier, poorer, and more illiterate.

Following the formula $L = \dfrac{O}{P}$, the most vulnerable nations are India, Pakistan, China, Indonesia, Iran, Turkey, Egypt, Colombia, and Peru.[2] They may have to face famine conditions within five to ten years. India, indeed, is already facing them.

Somewhat less vulnerable, says Dr. Raymond Ewell, are Burma, Thailand, the Philippines, Mexico, Chile, and native countries below the Sahara in Africa. Their deep crisis will come later, but the equation is against them too.

[2] Paper for Population Crisis Committee, 1966.

Let us look at typical nations on three continents: India (Asia), Egypt (Africa), and Mexico (Latin America.)

INDIA

We begin with the most vulnerable nation of all. Mr. Asoka Mehta, chief economic planner for the Indian Government, agrees with Dr. Ewell. The Indian birth rate, he says, is now 42, the death rate 19, which means a national increase of 23, or 11 million more persons a year. In reporting these figures, Mr. Mehta throws up his hands. The food supply, he says, is seriously inadequate, great quantities of grain must be imported, unemployment is severe, and the nation is short 70 million dwellings. Shortages will grow worse, he says, despite our efforts to develop the economy. Before plans can be effective the birth rate must be cut in half—down to around 20—not far from the present rate in both the United States and Russia.

Meanwhile as I write, in the province of Kerala, mobs are burning and rioting because they have little or no rice to eat. As rice eaters, they are psychically allergic to wheat, and even more allergic to the corn (maize) and sorghum which the U.S. has been shipping to India.

EGYPT

From Asia we turn to a vulnerable country in Africa. Egypt illustrates how, even when productivity is increased, the problem remains. In 1830 she had a population estimated at three million.[3] A dam was built in the Nile above Cairo, which irrigated more land and, with improvements in agricultural techniques, raised the population to 10 million by the end of the nineteenth century.

The first Aswan Dam was constructed by the British in

[3] Patrick Seale and Irene Beeson in *The New Republic,* May 7, 1966.

1902. It brought in another million acres for irrigation, and helped to treble the population to today's 30 million. Now the great new Aswan Dam, the building of which will flood priceless sculpture of the Pharaohs, is nearing completion. Can its irrigation canals feed Egypt's 800,000 babies a year, or will it encourage even more babies? At prevailing growth rates, population will double to 60 million by 1980, and the great monuments will have been inundated to no avail.

President Nasser, well aware of what has been happening to his country, had inaugurated a substantial birth control program before the Israeli War of 1967. New clinics are appearing, gleaming white against the dark mud huts of the Nile villages. There are, however, serious cultural and psychological difficulties. For centuries, Egyptian babies have been welcomed as insurance for the future support of their parents. A plentiful brood, moreover, has been cherished as proof of the father's virility. War losses in 1967 put additional strains on Egypt's economy.

MEXICO

In the early 1930's the population of this colorful country was estimated at 16 million. In 1966 it was 40 million. No fewer than 75 million people are predicted by 1980, if the current growth rate continues. Should it persist unabated, there would be 800 million Mexicans south of the Rio Grande a hundred years from now, exceeding the present population of China!

The birth rate in Mexico was around 50 per thousand in 1930, and is not much less today. But with the help of medical technology the death rate has dropped from 27 to 12. What is Mexico doing about her birth rate? Very little. During my visit there in 1966, I was told that the government was apathetic and the Church generally opposed to birth control, especially in the villages.

Mexico in the mid-1960's had perhaps the best economic record of any Latin-American nation, and was not much concerned with its demography. What really got attention, I found, was the rising gross national product. How long, however, can a prosperity in pesos cope with a 3.6 percent growth rate in people?

BIRTH CONTROL

In the late 1960's India appears on the brink of disaster, Egypt is but a few years away, and Mexico only a few years beyond that—*if current rates continue.* The vulnerable nations face a reckoning in the next decade. Will it be orderly or chaotic? The only orderly and permanent solution lies in the planned control of population. Planned control is not a new idea. The Greeks and the Romans practiced it from time to time by exposing babies, especially girl babies and those with physical defects. Other societies have led the aged off to die, with due ceremony. Crude methods of abortion and contraception are probably as old as the race.

The exposure of children and old people is repugnant today in all cultures, while abortion is repugnant in many. Infanticide is a crime, but is not unknown. The modern crime of so-called "child battering," in which distracted parents beat their children, sometimes to death, is increasingly reported by American social workers. There are far kinder ways to control population. Applied science, which brought on the crisis, is now hard at work seeking to mitigate it by new and improved techniques—oral pills, the uterine loop, the temporary sterilization of men and women. A postintercourse pill is in the laboratory. All this came into the headlines in 1965, when an area hitherto dark was suddenly illumined, and the public debate over the issue has remained active and growing.

The goal of the birth control movement is a balanced society where man and his environment are in reasonable equilibrium, where children are wanted and cared for. As we observed in the last chapter, if a given society desires a 70-year life span, with modern medicine and a low death rate, *it must limit its birth rate*. Fortunately, intelligent people throughout the world, like the chief planner of India, are beginning to grasp this simple logic.

The late Margaret Sanger was a pioneer in birth control and had the courage to go to jail for it. She began her crusade with a clinic in Brooklyn in 1916, not so much as a solution to world problems, as the result of personal problems she had known in her own family. In a Senate hearing in 1932 she was denounced as a corrupter of public morals, whose program "will rob the nation of military power, even for defensive purposes."

To her, the reform would liberate women from what amounted to biological slavery. Her mail was full of heartbreaking letters from mothers reduced to despair by continuous pregnancies, sick and hungry children. She was told of many cases where a woman died young from bearing too many babies, leaving a motherless brood. To Mrs. Sanger and her colleagues, birth control seemed to have a vital function, too, in preventing war—by reducing the "cannon fodder" of the military establishment. She finally became the honorary head of a great world movement—"Planned Parenthood—World Population," with a long list of prominent and distinguished sponsors, including ex-Presidents, publishers, cabinet members, and many physicians.[4]

Dr. John Rock, a gynecologist and a Catholic, who was instrumental in developing a safe oral pill, appeared before a

---

[4] Active promoters and sponsors in the U.S. now include ex-Presidents Eisenhower and Truman, President Johnson, General William H. Draper, Jr., Cass Canfield, Senators Ernest Gruening and Joseph Clark, Hugh Moore, Harry Emerson Fosdick, Dr. Mary S. Calderone, George Kennan, Marriner Eccles, Elmo Roper, Chester Bowles, Stewart Udall, John W. Gardner, and many more distinguished Americans.

Senate committee in 1965 to say: "The growth of population on this planet presents a lethal threat to all that civilization has achieved." In 1967 he took the position that failing birth control the United States had reached the limit of its ability to educate its children, while the underdeveloped nations, three-quarters of humanity, had already *exceeded* that limit. He was saying in effect that the family cannot adequately perpetuate the species in the face of the population explosion.

These are strong words, and they come from a Catholic doctor. For many years the Church has been the most formidable institution arrayed against contraceptives. Now the Church is ready to discuss the question, and an eminent Catholic layman of the Harvard Medical School is mixing pills. It is as if the Berlin Wall had suddenly been thrown down!

The United Nations, the World Bank, U.S. Government departments, the U.S. War on Poverty, Food-for-Freedom, and innumerable organizations here and abroad are now combining to carry on the work which Margaret Sanger so gallantly began. Programs, some of them ambitious, are under way in India, China, Egypt, Pakistan, South Korea, Taiwan, Kenya, Tunisia, and Turkey.

A Gallup poll in 1965 indicated that Americans are beginning to understand this crisis. Seventy percent of interviewed adults said that birth control information should be available to all married persons who want it; 50 percent went so far as to propose it for unmarried persons. A slim majority felt that population was a serious problem in the United States, and a larger majority felt it a serious world problem. Two-thirds believed that the federal government should aid states and cities with birth control programs. Educated respondents, ironically, were far ahead of the poorly educated in their replies, and of course it is the uneducated who need the information most.

Meanwhile Professor Robin Barlow of the University of

Michigan says that programs for malaria control should be accompanied by programs for birth control. Otherwise, he says, the economic gains of improved health "can be turned into an economic loss." (This is exactly what is happening in Mauritius.)

An energetic campaign has undoubtedly at last begun, but the total effect to date is hardly more than a launching pad. Robert C. Cook estimates that births, the world around, must be reduced by at least 20 million a year within a decade. This is a formidable goal. More than a billion adults in the Hungry World must be reached and be shown the techniques that are available. The total outlay for research so far is small—only a tiny fraction of the cost to put a man on the moon.

WILL MORE FOOD SAVE THE DAY?

The idea that all we need to do is to grow more food dies hard. More food postpones the crisis; *it does not solve it*. Even with the most advanced technical aid, the supply of food in the world cannot hope to keep up with population at present rates of growth; Malthus stands vindicated. In 1965, when national food stocks were near their peak, the United States had enough surplus wheat in storage to feed the world for just two weeks. More food can certainly be grown, it can be dredged from the sea; eventually it can even be synthesized. These processes, however, will take time, and enormous amounts of capital, while the effect can only be temporary.

According to a U.S. Government task force, in the five years from 1960 to 1965 population in the Hungry World increased twice as fast as its output of food. Before World War II, low-energy areas exported large amounts of grain, net, to the high-energy nations. Now the net traffic is moving the other way. To make matters worse, prices have been rising for manufactured goods imported by the poorer countries, while prices of the raw materials which they grow and export have been declining.

Secretary of Agriculture Orville L. Freeman sums it up:

There are three basic benchmarks to which the rate of increase in food production can be usefully related: *first,* the rate of increase needed to keep pace with population growth; *second,* the rate of increase needed to attain target rates of economic growth while maintaining stable prices; *third,* the rate needed to eliminate the serious malnutrition common to most of the developing countries. By all three criteria, the rate of food increase has been inadequate. . . . *We are losing the war on hunger.*

THE CASE OF JAPAN

Before we despair, however, let us look at a great nation which has reduced its birth rate by half in the last 15 years, and pared its growth rate to that of Western Europe. Japan has demonstrated that population can be controlled, at least in a disciplined society.

Japan must support 100 million people in an area about the size of California, only one-sixth of which is arable. After her defeat in World War II, soldiers came home from all over the Pacific and the birth rate jumped. A serious food shortage loomed, and something had to be done. In 1948 the Diet adopted the "Eugenic Protective Law," with competent medical advice, and the announced purpose of promoting family welfare. The effect on the whole social structure was destined to be profound.

A desperate situation called for a desperate remedy. Abortion was made legal; one gynecologist could sanction the operation. The law applied to very poor families, to women who were ill, and to victims of rape. Legal abortions rose to a peak of more than a million in 1955 and then declined, as contraceptives began in part to replace them. One result was the virtual elimination of illegitimate births.

By the late 1950's hundreds of health centers were established throughout Japan to give contraceptive information and supplies, while 50,000 nurses were specially trained. Big Business cooperated effectively by setting up clinics along with company housing. Courses in birth control became as popular as courses in cooking and child care. Businessmen did not fail to notice, furthermore, that the factory accident rate declined. They account for it by the fact that workers slept better, with fewer crying babies in the small Japanese homes.

By 1964 the birth rate had fallen from 34 per thousand to 17—*cut in half in 15 years.* This compared with an average European birth rate of 18, an American and a Russian rate of just over 20. The Japanese death rate also declined along with everybody else's, but even so the growth rate fell below one percent a year, about that of Western Europe. (Japan was included with Western Europe in Dr. Keyfitz's group 1, cited earlier.)

Japan is now dealing with a labor shortage, the reverse of unemployment. The number of young people coming on the job market is going down—while in the United States the number is going up. This has forced Japanese businessmen to pay higher wages. Older workers, meanwhile, are no longer "fired at 40"—or 50 or 60. The retirement age is up, too, along with an increase in training programs for both old and young.

In short, Japan has taught the world two important lessons: the benefits to the economy of a low growth rate in people, and, even more significant, the proof that a whole population can be deliberately planned and controlled. We must remember, however, that Japan is a special case—a high-energy society in low-energy Asia. To do what Japan has done requires a literate, disciplined people, without strong superstitions, or theological principles governing the biology of reproduction.

OUR GRAVEST PROBLEM

Many students consider the population crisis the trend most to be feared and outmaneuvered. It is not alone the problem of the Hungry World; we are all in this together, rich nations and poor alike. One can anticipate, however, a vigorous attempt, by people with little knowledge and imagination, to seal off the poor nations, halt foreign aid programs, and let two-thirds of mankind starve its way to some kind of primitive equilibrium. I doubt the success of any such movement, however vocal its advocates. It is too late; technology has bound us too firmly together. Telstar lights the television sets of all the continents, no nation is self-supporting, jet planes weave in and out of every capital, the United Nations is a growing symbol of a world united in material fact. One might even hazard the guess that the most urgent business of the United Nations for some years to come will not be so much the policing of cease-fire agreements as promoting smaller families.

The total world-wide growth rate is the result of the birth rate less the death rate, disregarding in- and out-migration. If a given community had 1,000 souls at the beginning of the year, and 50 were born and 40 died during the year, there would be 1,010 people at the end. This is an increase of 10 per thousand, or a growth rate of one percent.

This rate can be raised by improved medical care acting on the death rate and making people live longer. It can be reduced harmlessly by birth control, or violently by famine, plague, and war. A thermonuclear war, however, would probably poison the pool of human genes by massive fallout, with effects disastrous beyond calculation.

The long-term goal becomes increasingly clear: it is an average of not much over two children per family. (Ireland for the moment has a negative growth rate; so has East Germany, doubtless due to out-migration.) The result will be a *growth rate close to zero,* if a steady-state world is to be won.

This is probably the most important finding in my whole study; a growth rate close to zero.

Let Arnold Toynbee have the last word. He told the World Food Congress in Washington in June, 1963:

We must aim at a figure that will allow a substantial part of our time and energy to be spent, not on keeping ourselves alive, but on making human life a more civilized affair than we have succeeded in making it so far.

5

OUR SHRINKING LIVING SPACE

WE HAVE observed the population curve, which seems to be leading to crisis. In this chapter we will observe the environment in which people must live for a long time to come. Many years ago I wrote a book about the American land. After presenting a good deal of evidence about forests, grasslands, soils, silting, water pollution, erosion, and wild life, I said:

A continent is *situs,* a place to live and so more than a bread factory. People do not make continents, continents make people. The age-long strength of Russia is due to her latitude, climate, resources and sweep . . . the strength of our nation is due to the continent of North America. It has molded us, nourished us, fed its abundant vitality into our veins. We are its children, lost and homeless without its strong arms about us. Shall we destroy it?[1]

If I try to answer that question today after years of close attention, I must say yes and no, with rather more emphasis on the "yes"; we are destroying it. True, the conservation measures sponsored by Franklin Roosevelt, who loved the land, and before him by Theodore Roosevelt and Gifford Pinchot, have won some victories. The galloping destruction of American forests has been checked as perpetual-yield forestry replaces the slash and burn of the old lumber barons.

[1] *Rich Land, Poor Land.* See Reading List.

Soil erosion has been checked with the skillful methods of the U.S. Soil Conservation Service, and replaced over great areas by plowing on the contours—as any cross-country flight will quickly make evident. The Tennessee Valley Authority has brought better patterns of land use to a great river basin.

Some of these gains, however, have been more than offset by the country's growth and prosperity. Bulldozers carving out superhighways and subdivisions are eating away topsoil and vegetation, and so increasing floods. The pollution of American waters is worse than ever, and so is open-pit mining, which produces a veritable lunar landscape. The correlation between high prosperity and mountains of refuse is not only direct, but ascends at an accelerating rate. In addition, some startling new techniques for destroying North America as a habitable environment have recently appeared, such as sonic boom.

Although the United States has undisputed leadership in laying waste its natural resources, all high-energy societies tend to follow the pattern. Even the careful Germans have not stopped the gross pollution of the Rhine. One fears that the poor countries will tend to do likewise, if and when they achieve affluence.

ONE-EIGHTH ONLY

It is sobering to remember that only about 12 percent of the surface of the earth is fit for human habitation. That surface has been called a "thin lamination." We live between an ocean of air above and a rocky crust beneath. The air must be reasonably pure if we are to breathe, the soil must be arable if we are to eat, the water must be clean if we are to drink. Two-thirds of the globe's surface is salt water, while polar ice, tundra, high mountains, deserts, swamps, and rain forests reduce the land on which we can live with any comfort to not more than one-eighth of the earth's surface.

How many of us in affluent societies have any conception of the meaning of these limitations? If we do not like where we are, we get in the car and go somewhere else. Yet living space is only a small part of the planet's surface, and now a series of technologies on the loose are squeezing it smaller. The man-land density is increasing, not only because land is limited and population is going up, but because more and more of the land is becoming unfit for human living. We have sturdily refused to accept our place in nature. "If any biological system," observed Dr. Dickerman Richards of Columbia, "were to have the kind of chaos our social system has, it would not survive five minutes."

Every once in a while, amid the stupendous chaos of ramming a new superhighway across the continent, the motorist sees a lonely frame house surrounded by great mounds of uprooted earth and blasted rock. It has been abandoned by its owner, but the bulldozers have not got around to pulling it down. This may be a fair analogy for what is happening to all our homes: the bulldozers have not got around to pulling them down. Day by day the roar grows louder. When they do get around, where shall we live?

EIGHT ASSAULTS ON LIVING SPACE

That modern dinosaur, the bulldozer, went into mass production during World War II, which it helped to win. Today it is a familiar sight, driven by an impetuous young man in a state of high exhilaration, leveling hills, obliterating brooks, toppling large trees. No forest, meadow, or shore is safe, as it roots out the habitat of plants and animals, including, in the last analysis, man. The bulldozer, indeed, can be taken as a symbol of a shrinking environment. It represents a technological trend only less menacing than the growth of population and the arms race.

We could begin the analysis far up in space, even at the

moon. The military have splendid plans for burning up a continent with missiles fired from the moon. Then we could descend to the stratosphere and find more trouble, especially radioactive fallout. Descend again to normal atmosphere and note what is perhaps the most acute threat of all at present, air pollution. Then down to earth for disturbances in the balance of nature, governing land and water. But it may be better to arrange the assaults by their current urgency. There are at least eight of them, as follows:

1. *Pollutants of the air*

Water can be channeled in aqueducts and mains, but not so air. New York City is now discovering that any real control of smog is hopeless if it can roll across the bay from New Jersey on prevailing west winds. It bloweth where it listeth, to be sure, but it must carry whatever cargo presents itself. A raw mixture of carbon, sulphur, nitrogen compounds, water vapor, and stockyard odors hangs constantly over the Jersey meadows, awaiting transport.

The word "smog," coined as a combination of "smoke" and "fog," has lost its original meaning. Los Angeles, the most publicized producer, has little smoke today and almost no fog. The term, however, is apparently here to stay and the definition must be expanded. It now refers to any condition of the air we breathe that offers a danger to health—from a slight headache to a fatal coma.

Smog seldom becomes serious without the condition known as "temperature inversion," where hot air does *not* rise and blow away as it normally should. The inversion sits like a lid over the landscape. In certain geographic areas the warm air, by causes not yet well understood, is prevented at times from rising, and any impurities stay in it, keeping foul air at nose level.[2]

The inversion is not caused by a city as such. The Los

[2] Following Dr. Donald E. Carr. See Reading List.

Angeles area undoubtedly suffered from it long before people settled there. Some cities have spells of inversion, others do not. Dublin does not, thanks to much wind and rain. Inversion has been noted in Tokyo, Paris, Leningrad, New York, Buenos Aires, Mexico City, Sydney, San Francisco, among others. It can even be found in the middle of the Kansas prairie. Inversion plus pollution killed 12,000 Londoners in 1952—the estimate of excess deaths due to a smog in which visibility was reduced to three feet. Inversion killed 20 and made 6,000 very sick in Donora, Pennsylvania, in 1948. London had another attack in 1956, and again in 1962. New York had excess deaths from inversion in 1953, 1963, and, with enormous publicity, and no little irony, on Thanksgiving Day, 1966. In the Japanese town of Yokkaichi, children play in the school yards equipped with gas masks.[3] Scientists suspect, says *Time,* that thousands of deaths in cities around the world can be linked to air pollution. It is particularly hard on lung patients. It is hard, too, on plants and trees. Certain nursery crops can no longer be grown where air pollution is heavy.

When inversion clamps down its lid, trouble comes for everyone who breathes. It comes in two forms, and from two major sources. One form is the visible particles of carbon dirt, coating the windowsill, which are known to all city-dwellers. The other form, and far more serious, is invisible gas; it accounts for some 90 percent of all air pollution. The major source for a hundred years has been smoke and gas from factory chimneys, where coal and oil are burned. Now, an even greater producer is the rear end of an automobile. Los Angeles, the prize example of inversion because of the city's encircling mountains, has long since compelled industry to use

---

[3] *Time* has a picture of them in its issue of January 27, 1967, together with full-page color photographs of many cities wreathed in sulphur dioxide.

fuels with low sulphur content, but "smog" is worse than ever. Why? Because there are more cars than ever.

Stop-start driving in congested areas releases, along with carbon monoxide (a favorite compound for suicides), various hydrocarbons and nitrogen oxides, and the higher the engine compression, the more perverse they become. No gadget so far designed is able to do more than somewhat reduce the exhaust danger, and Dr. Carr doubts if an effective gadget can be designed.

Meanwhile Dr. Philip A. Leighton, professor emeritus of chemistry at Stanford, concentrating on the nitrogen oxides (which seem to be the most insidious of the lot), has made the following calculation: A full-sized American car cruising at 60 miles an hour emits about three liters of nitrogen oxides per minute. To dilute this blast to safe breathing limits requires more than 60 million liters of fresh air per minute, "a rate which is enough to supply the average breathing requirements, over the same period, of five to 10 million people." This causes Dr. Leighton to wonder if the resource which will really force the control of population, will be not land, food or water, but *air* . . . sixty million liters of fresh air per car per minute.[4]

Here is a dilemma indeed. We have been quite unable to prevent bigger and better traffic jams, which produce bigger doses of nitrogen oxides. We managed to ban the testing of nuclear bombs in the atmosphere because of fallout, but to ban the burning of gasoline promises to be a much more serious business. It would not only bring Detroit and the petroleum industry in on the double-quick, but create a great outcry from the public, in defense of its most cherished artifact. John W. Gardner, Secretary of Health, Education, and Welfare, showed real courage when he declared at a 1966 conference that the gasoline automobile and the welfare of the

[4] *Geographic Review,* April, 1966.

American people are on a collision course: "None of us would wish to sacrifice the convenience of private passenger automobiles, but the day may come when we may have to trade convenience for survival."

The following figures furnish eloquent proof of the dilemma:

ANNUAL AIR POLLUTANTS IN THE UNITED STATES[5]

Millions of Tons

From transportation engines, cars, trucks, etc.	85
manufacturing plants	22
electric power plants	15
space heating	8
refuse burning	3
Total	133

That means more than half a ton descending on every man, woman, and child in the country, every year.

2. *Fallout*

High above the exhaust fumes, fallout from nuclear explosions circles the globe in the stratosphere, gradually sifting down. It does not confine its donations to Los Angeles, New York, or London, but distributes them impartially to all mankind. True, the atmosphere of the planet, extending about 30 miles up, has been assailed with substances harmful to human beings ever since volcanoes erupted, or large forest fires were set by lightning, or certain rock formations gave off radiation. Such emissions were "Acts of God," assaults on living things by nature. In the last few years, however, man himself has led the radioactive assault.

Following the Test Ban Treaty of 1963, nuclear explosions have been conducted underground by the United States, Russia, and Britain, but the other members of the "Nuclear Club," France and China, have continued to throw poisons into the air we breathe, and to coat with poison some of the plants we

[5] United States Department of the Interior *Year Book,* 1966.

eat. The danger is certainly not building up at the rate that prevailed before the test ban, but there is plenty of toxic matter still aloft. Dr. Linus Pauling, Nobel laureate in chemistry, has predicted that millions of defective babies will be born over the years as a result of fallout which descended before 1963.

3. Controlling the weather

Contrails from the proposed supersonic airliners may upset weather by accident, but both the military and the rainmakers have larger designs. The former want to make weather very unpleasant for an enemy, while the latter want, for example, to alleviate such droughts as afflicted the New York area in the 1960's, and hopefully to dissolve hurricanes with silver iodide.

The National Science Foundation at Washington, however, considers tampering with the climate about on a par with a nuclear explosion. The Foundation calls for a good deal more research before swinging into action. This should include a study of the biological, social, economic, political, and legal effects of changing the established climate in a given area. The last promises to occupy platoons of lawyers and judges, both national and international. What if Canada wants rain for its wheat crop, while the state of Washington, on the other side of the boundary, is inundated by floods? Who wins when skiers and resort owners want snow and motorists want clear roads?

4. Noise

Sound waves traverse the air, and when they have unpleasant effects on eardrums, can be called a kind of air pollution. A whisper is rated by the sound engineers at 20 decibels, ordinary conversation is rated at 60, factory operations and cocktail parties compete at 85 to 90.[6] If you are subjected to 120

---

[6] Harland Manchester in the *National Civic Review*, September, 1964. Traffic noise on New York sidewalks is rated at 103 decibels; subway coaches at 100.

decibels for any length of time, you are likely to suffer permanent damage to your hearing.

It is estimated that average sound levels in the U.S. have increased by some 30 decibels in recent years. Indeed, why not? It seems a modest estimate. A few decades ago one might lie in his hammock in once-rural Connecticut, where I now live, and hear the croaking of frogs, the singing of birds, the lowing of cattle, the barking of dogs over the hill, perhaps a neighbor pounding nails, the occasional clatter of hooves on the dirt road, the complaint of a heavily loaded wagon, punctuated by the crack of a whip and a cry of "Giddap, you Dobbin!" That is about all he would hear.

Now, sitting on an aluminum garden chair where the hammock used to be, what does one hear? Some of the old sounds to be sure—birds and dogs—but no horses, no creaking wagons, no lowing cattle. You hear the woosh of car after car on the blacktop, the laboring gears of a 20-ton truck hauling sand and gravel to the new superhighway, the roar of motorcycles, a loudspeaker dispensing *Pagliacci* from a neighbor's house, a power lawn mower chattering, the rhythmic thump of a well driller, the screech of power saws clearing the telephone line, the grunt of bulldozers as they tear out a new subdivision, the wailing of an ambulance siren en route to the Danbury Hospital. These are not simultaneous decibels, to be sure, but they are all sounds I have entered in my notebook as occurring within a few hours.

In the troubled air, meanwhile, mingled with the alarms of crows, you can hear trainer planes from the Danbury Airport, helicopters from Sikorsky's, big four-engine props heading for La Guardia, and mammoth jets from across the Atlantic coming down in thunder to Kennedy Airport 50 miles away. This is what you hear in my rustic retreat today—with the bright promise of a "sonic carpet" descending tomorrow.

The sonic carpet is a truly uproarious item in the curve of

technology. The term has been used by a Swedish engineer, after a study of sonic boom was made in Oklahoma in 1965.[7] The "carpet" delimits the broad swath of living space made momentarily uninhabitable by sonic boom. When a plane goes faster than the speed of sound (640 miles an hour), it may enter a less turbulent area in the sky, but the turbulence below becomes fantastic. It generates a minor earthquake, breaking windows, dishes, and nervous systems from coast to coast.

Dr. Lundberg reports that the Oklahoma effects were worse than expected. The boom carpet, he says, is between 50 and 80 miles wide, so that cities, suburbs, and countryside alike are blasted. Furthermore, he says, the boom is intensified by certain atmospheric conditions and can be more than doubled by reflection from walls; it seems that the decibels bounce. There will be intolerable insomnia for all in the boom carpet, much physical damage, and many serious accidents. "The comfort and safety of millions of people will be sacrificed to the convenience of a few travelers."

5. *The pollution of waters*

There is no major river in the United States which is not grossly polluted. People still drink the water after heavy chlorination, though many buy expensive bottled water, even for tea and coffee. The alarm some of us raised a generation ago has had very little effect.

The despoliation of American rivers is an old and dishonorable story, but lately the fate of Lake Erie has held the headlines. President Johnson made a special journey in 1966 to inspect the desolation. In the same week came a story from Russia that Lake Baikal in Siberia was threatened with the chemical wastes of a vast new pulp mill complex. Russian conservationists promptly moved to head off the disaster.

Lake Erie is a large inland sea, convering 2,600 square

[7] Dr. B. K. O. Lundberg in *Bulletin of the Atomic Scientists,* February, 1965.

miles, large enough, one would expect, to be proof against any trash men might throw into it. Not so. From Detroit on the west to Buffalo on the east, city sewage and the offscourings of industry flush filth into waters which millions of American have long depended upon for drinking, swimming, fishing, and boating. The bathing beaches are now closed, and the boat liveries bankrupt. *Newsweek* in April, 1965, tells the sad story:

> Lake Erie is dying. Called *eutrophication,* this death comes ironically from too much nutrition, as when an obese man eats until his heart quits. Nitrogen, phosphorus and filth in the lake feed immense blooms of green algae that burn up oxygen at the lake's bottom needed by higher forms of life . . . useful water life has already been smothered. . . . Revitalization will require more than elaborate pollution-control schemes, for *eutrophication,* once started, feeds on itself.

At the other end of New York State, to the east, lies the Hudson River, in almost as sad a plight. Sixteen cities, from Troy southward to New York Harbor, contribute raw sewage, while other towns give it only a sketchy treatment. The U.S. Public Health Service estimates that the Hudson gets the waste of 10 million people. "That is what one would expect if, for these 158 miles, both banks of the river were lined solidly with outhouses."[8]

Additional wastes pour into the Hudson from scores of factories: fibers from paper mills, grease and flesh from slaughterhouses, dyes from chemical plants, chemicals from drug makers, acids from metal-processing, oils from automobile paint shops . . . a long way from the year 1609 when Henry Hudson found the river "clear, blue and wonderful to taste."

The Mississippi River, down which Huck Finn and Jim floated on their immortal raft in the old steamboat days, has

[8] Peter T. White in the *New York Times Magazine,* July 17, 1966.

been equally despoiled. Huck and Jim would not relish going overboard for a swim today. Meanwhile pesticides have been killing the few types of fish which can survive the standard load of pollution. A serious difficulty is that sewer mains and storm drains are combined in most American cities. A big rain is often too much for the sewage treatment plant, if there is one, and the excess overflows into the river along with the storm water.

When the rivers with their heavy burdens come down to the coast, bathing beaches, oyster beds, and lobster pots are abandoned as the bacteria count goes up. Nor are the rivers alone the source of coastal grief. Oil dumped from oceangoing tankers comes washing ashore, ruining the beaches for bathers, preventing shellfish from breeding, and killing gulls and terns. When a bird's feathers are coated with oil, the poor creature can neither swim nor fly, and must die of starvation.

6. *Water supply*

As in the case of air, the world's water supply is strictly limited. Only 3 percent of the total is fresh water, and most of this is locked in polar ice caps and mountain glaciers. Modern cities want more water for air-conditioning units; farmers want more for irrigation. Arizona, for instance, now depends on underground waters for cities and farms and the water table is steadily falling—some 300,000 acres of cropland have been abandoned. Unless nuclear desalting of sea water becomes practical within a decade, a lot of people may have to move out of Arizona. Meanwhile California, Arizona, and Mexico are in a chronic legal battle as to which gets how much water from the Colorado River. A more sanguinary battle goes on between Jordan and Israel as to who controls the waters of the Jordan River.

There is, of course, a hopeful note in the coming desalting of sea water by nuclear energy. Intensive R & D is bringing costs per gallon down so rapidly that some coastal areas will surely receive a new and permanent supply of fresh water within a decade. How far inland desalted water can economically be pumped is another question. A further optimistic note from R & D is the recycling of used and dirty water. It is not particularly pleasant to contemplate, but the engineers say that it will taste all right. Foul water is recycled by nature too, but in a larger and slower operation.

7. *Pollution of the land*

> Beside the road day-lilies grow
> Amid the beer cans, row on row.

There are worse pollutants than empty beer cans, but in America, at least, few things are more visible as one drives along the roads, except, of course, billboards. I pick up the cans, flung gaily from cars which pass in the night, every morning around my front gate. They are a symbol of the stupendous piles of junk and refuse which our affluent society throws off.

In *God's Own Junkyard,* Peter Blake superbly documents the trend—with the most dreadful photographs. One reason why junk grows faster than people is the up-and-coming merchandising of the container—the idea being to sell the package rather than what is in it. A comfortable 60 percent of Americans are now in the affluent class, with access to all the good things of life. This does not impress Marya Mannes: "Americans had better be told," she says, "that the more people attain the good things of life, the less good resides in these things." The American Academy of Sciences adds a statistical note. In 1920 the average American threw away 2.75 pounds of refuse a day. In 1965 he threw away eight pounds. "As the earth becomes more crowded, there is no longer any 'away.' One person's trash basket is another's living space."

The junk yards, the roadsides, and the beaches can someday hopefully be cleaned up—perhaps by using manpower made obsolete by automation—*if* enough people are sufficiently revolted by the "effluent age." Soil erosion, however, will take longer to heal. It is not so much the up-and-down plowing which causes it now as the runoff from blacktop highways. Soil, as well as air and water, can be so poisoned as to render it unfit for growing food. This condition results, says the U.S. Department of Agriculture, from adding waste products to the soil faster than they decompose. Pesticides also contribute to soil pollution, and so does fallout. A kind of somber cooperation exists where, says the Department, "air pollutants—such as automobile exhausts, industrial smoke and radioactive fallout—ultimately become soil pollutants as well."

The most spectacular destruction of the good earth is, of course, open-pit mining for coal and other minerals. Without careful and expensive replacement of the soil when the operation is over, nothing may ever grow there again. By contrast, in Germany a mine cannot be opened unless plans are first filed to heal the wound, with severe penalties for their neglect.

The United States lags far behind Europe in protecting its land, but the President's Advisory Committee on Environmental Pollution makes the sound point that *there should be no right to pollute*. Antipollution measures should take their place along with public schools as a mandatory public service. In due course industry must include the costs of pollution control together with materials and labor.

8. *Outer space*

Above the land, the waters, and the air lies outer space, safe from all human interference until a certain day in 1945 when the first nuclear bomb was exploded in a New Mexico desert. Its ancient peace is now violated so frequently that someone has proposed, not entirely humorously, that the United Nations send up a platoon of space policemen to control the traffic.

If space is ever used in thermonuclear war, it will be quite possible, scientists say, to incinerate a substantial fraction of a continent by firestorm. We remember Mr. Khrushchev's threat when he was head of the Russian state: "Germany will burn like a candle." Germany can be burned even more efficiently now, with the latest nuclear hardware.

Real damage, rather than speculative, occurred when the U.S. exploded a device in outer space a few years ago. It broke up the so-called Van Allen belt, which guards the earth from too much radiation. Scientists, including Dr. Van Allen himself, were shocked by this reckless act.

THE SPIRIT OF ST. FRANCIS

From the beer can tossers to the open-pit miners to the disrupters of the Van Allen belt, the trend continues almost unabated. Not only in North America but all over the world, living space is under concentrated attack.

No creature purposely destroys its home, and the only excuse for Homo sapiens is that most of us are still unaware of what we are doing. In our ignorance we suppose that air, water, and land are unlimited. We have in fact become, as the great ecologist Paul Sears once said, a kind of geologic force, more destructive in the long run than hurricanes or earthquakes.

This behavior is deep-rooted, and some students, such as Professor Lynn T. White, trace it back down the centuries to the very foundations of our Judeo-Christian culture. Though Copernicus demonstrated the fallacy of the Ptolemaic system, which had made man the center of the universe, with sun, planets, and the stars revolving deferentially around him, the theologians of the time were far from being defeated. They continued to regard man as the sole possessor of the planet, with dominion over the fish of the sea, the fowl of the air, and over every living thing that moveth upon the earth, and, to make it final, dominion over all the earth. Only St. Francis of

Assisi seriously challenged this doctrine; he was bold enough to believe that other living creatures had some rights.

One might add, in all deference, that our children's children have some rights too.

The pollutants now at large—in space, in the air and water, and on land—are not confined to any one city or state or nation. The Van Allen belt fiasco affected the whole world. The "air shed" of New York City includes at least four states and may drift into Canada. Remedial measures and laws which apply to a single political division will be mostly unavailing. The protection of living space is a matter for the federal government in Washington, on one level; for all the countries of North America, or of Europe, on another level; for the United Nations on a planetary level. It is evident that we must make our peace with nature herself, as well as with the fact of thermonuclear bombs.

6

MEGALOPOLIS

WHEN at the dawn of what we are pleased to call "civiliza-tion," men first began to build cities, it was an early variety of technology that enabled them to do so. Without a dependable supply of water and consequent drainage, without a storable grain, without some means for recording transactions, people could not have lived together in permanent towns. These de-vices were gradually extended and improved. Each extension allowed the city to grow larger in area and in population, and the extensions, which I can no longer bring myself to call improvements, continue to this day. An early city may have been able to support 20,000, while London, New York, and Tokyo today are not far short of 10 million.

So huge are these modern conglomerations that they have laid claim to the term "megalopolis," or supercity, including not only the downtown area but the surrounding suburbs. Into the city, people who once lived on the land are now pouring, both in rich countries and in poor, to create vast new prob-lems of housing, slums, traffic, pollution, crime, water supply, taxes, and waste disposal. In affluent societies, at the same time, the middle class is pouring out into the suburbs, seeking open space and better schools for the children. As a result, the Census population of most large American cities is not in-creasing by much, though the whole urban field is growing rapidly. New York City remains at eight million, while the area where I live near New York is up 60 percent in a decade.

THE NEW YORK "URBAN FIELD"

Let us take New York as a leading representative of the trend. I have lived for most of my life in the area, in what the city planners are beginning to call the "urban field"—by analogy to the magnetic field in physics. It includes the core city, in this case Manhattan Island, and its rings of boroughs and suburbs and exurbs. I used to be proud of this great, soaring city, guarded by the Statue of Liberty in its majestic harbor, but now I avoid going into it unless my business is very urgent. In recent years, New York, like Job, has suffered one affliction after another, causing Murray Kempton to say:

> In the slow, dreary business of urban decay, New Yorkers will be remembered as are the Londoners in the early 1940s. We are the combat soldiers of urban catastrophe. . . . Under Republicans as under Democrats, to live in New York is to be condemned to one cosmic civic disaster after another every few months.[1]

The strike of the transit unions in 1966 against the city-owned Transit Authority encouraged 850,000 private automobiles to enter and hopefully leave Manhattan. In these "rush hours" traffic moved like a glacier throughout the day and far into the night. The cars crawled bumper to bumper in lines as long as three miles, generally with only two persons to a car. (In a normal day, 600,000 cars crowd in with an even lower average load.) Fire trucks and ambulances could not make their way through the mass of steel and chromium; doctors could not reach their patients; hospitals had to postpone operations as blood banks gave out.

Six weeks before this "cosmic civic disaster," because of the

---

[1] *New Republic,* January 15, 1966. If this seems extreme, *Fortune* magazine has more than emphasized it with its story, "A City Destroying Itself" (September, 1964).

malfunctioning of a small mechanism called a relay, electric power failed all over the Northeast for many hours. In New York City 800,000 subway riders were suddenly trapped underground, and untold thousands in elevators between floors. Hundreds of the latter were chopped out by firemen. The airports were abandoned and all railroad commuting traffic ceased. Commuters, photographed as they slept on the floor of Grand Central Station, looked like the dead after an air raid. Before the power failure came an acute water crisis, with city reservoirs going dry;[2] before that, a newspaper strike which lasted 100 days. After the transit strike came two air pollution emergencies, and after that a blizzard, which brought all motorized surface transportation to a standstill.

Smog to rival Los Angeles has steadily been building up in New York, whose sulphur-dioxide count leads the nation. The crime rate increases faster than the population, and in some districts vigilantes have been organized by terrified citizens to protect themselves against the murders, rapes, and robberies which the police are unable to control. Slums in Harlem and Brooklyn are torn by race riots in the hot summer, and nobody in his right mind dares to walk in the parks at night.

The middle class moves en masse to the suburbs, and industry moves with them, precipitating a financial crisis as the tax base erodes. A million people are on relief in New York despite the nationwide prosperity of the mid-sixties. The very rich together with the very poor, who are mostly Negroes and Puerto Ricans, stay behind as the middle class departs.

Joseph Lyford, after living for five years in the slums of Harlem, has given a searing account of what is happening to children there:

We are in the middle of a system that requires more and more human beings to grow up as welfare babies. I mean the piling up of

[2] At the time when the water supply was critical, the affluent thing to have in the suburbs was a swimming pool.

children in the dark parts of our cities and leaving them to rot. . . .
I have looked at many scores of children who do not look back at
me because they cannot. They do not see or hear the way a human
being should be able to see or hear . . . sometimes, if you watch the
process, you may see the exact moment when a child gives up the
struggle. . . .[3]

The first U.S. Census in 1790 showed 95 percent of Americans in rural areas, in the green country, where presumably
they could see and hear as human beings should. Philip M.
Hauser estimates that as late as 1800 only 3 percent of the
world's population was living in cities. The 1960 U.S. Census
found 70 percent of Americans in the urban field. This trend
is world-wide and "is unprecedented in its implication for
changing the behavior and attitudes of man." Cultural lag,
says Hauser, prevents us from boldly facing the change. Our
belief systems are still oriented around the self-sufficient
farmer of a century and more ago.

The density of Manhattan is 75,000 persons per square
mile, a figure which depersonalizes face-to-face contacts. The
callous "go ahead and jump" reaction to would-be suicides on
window ledges becomes normal. Who lives in the next apartment and who cares? Who cares about welfare babies, or a
million on relief? Megalopolis is creating a condition where
the density is greater than human nature can deal with. The
result is "alienation," the "Lonely Crowd," the loss of friendly
person-to-person contacts.

One must ask, however, if this has not always been true of
cities, from Sumer to Babylon to Rome? No qualified sociologist ever reported firsthand on pre-machine-age cities, but one
can hazard a reasonable guess. They certainly had dreadful
slums as well as spacious plazas, and alienation may well have
been endemic. But all cities before, say, 1850, had to be relatively small by modern standards because of the problem of

[3] *The Airtight Cage.* See Reading List.

human waste. Cities were not equipped with the sanitary facilities to take care of it. Sanitation was purely a handicraft operation. Just think about it seriously for a few minutes; it will be unpleasant but educational. What did the good burghers do with garbage and human wastes? Modern engineering has solved that problem by creating another one—the gross pollution of rivers and estuaries.

Fortune commented on the Pan Am Building, the largest office building in the world, jammed up against the Grand Central Station in mid-Manhattan, with these words:

> Traffic still moves. The thousands of workers have been absorbed in the morning and nightly flood of subway riders. The noon-time scramble for lunch-counter space is more frantic but somehow the mob gulps hamburgers in 15 minute shifts. The sidewalks are packed but not quite impassable. All that has happened really is that life has become more unpleasant for countless people. The critics were not wrong to attack the Pan Am Building as an architectural and sociological atrocity. They simply underestimated the capacity of New Yorkers to endure inhuman pressures.

New York is breath-taking as one flies in from Europe, with the morning sun on its tall, white towers. At 40,000 feet one does not see the frustrations on the streets below. To look at the chaos of those streets and the people in them is to realize how limited are dollar statistics and the gross national product as indices of the good life. "American cities," says the *New York Times,* "are turning into collection points for the bulk of the nation's social ills, while they remain generators of national wealth."

At the height of the transit strike in 1966, with not a bus or subway train in operation and the streets choked with private cars, Art Buchwald wrote a famous column. He assumed that matters had come to such a pass that the City Fathers had decided to sell Manhattan Island back to the Indians for

$24—the original purchase price paid by the Dutch in 1626.

An authentic Indian chief is located, Buchwald continues, but negotiations are conducted with some difficulty. American Indians are celebrated for their skill in modern steel construction, and the chief is at work on a new skyscraper high above Park Avenue. The offer is made vertically upward from the sidewalk, but the chief shakes his head.

"How about four dollars down, and four dollars a month?"

"Nope."

The chief returns to his welding; New York City is not vendible.

When citizens can no longer take the "inhuman pressures" which *Fortune* depicts, how vendible will it be then?

"THE LOVED ONE" AGAIN

The automobile has not merely taken over the street; it has dissolved the living tissues of the city. Its appetite for space is insatiable; moving and parked, it devours urban land, leaving the buildings as mere islands of habitable space in a sea of dangerous traffic . . . gas-filled, noisy and hazardous, our streets have become the most inhumane landscapes in the world.[4]

The standard American car occupies about 100 square feet of space. As a vehicle for commuters it carries an average of 1.5 persons. Equal area in a bus or a subway car can carry up to 30 persons. These two are all the figures we need to show why traffic in American cities makes no sense. Taxis, trucks, and buses could probably be tolerated in the core city, despite street patterns laid out for pedestrians and horses—especially if many trucks were routed at night. But to date it is stoutly maintained that a private motorist has an inalienable right to rush through the city's core at the highest speed he can get away with, and that the duty of the government is to build

[4] James Marsten Fitch, professor of architecture, before the Academy of Political Science, 1960.

ever more highways, freeways, bridges, and tunnels to get him into town, and ever more parking lots to use when he gets there.

Los Angeles is the city furthest gone in its devotion to the loved one. Its tangle of freeways, leaping over and under one another in a gigantic cats' cradle, has reached a point where almost two-thirds of all downtown land has been surrendered to highways and parking lots. On the remaining one-third, people scuttle for their lives, not always with success. The pedestrian is a land animal on his way to extinction.

Proposals for mass transit by bus, subway, and railroad, to replace the private car, are met by the mass opposition of Detroit, of local car dealers, the American Automobile Association, highway contractors, parking lot operators, the gasoline, tire, cement and asphalt industries, traffic light dealers— indeed by all the impacted and vested interests which have grown up around city traffic. Perhaps adequate parking could be provided for shoppers and trippers, but for commuters with their two peak loads it is impossible. "Congestion is quietly accepted as the cheapest device for discouraging private drivers, and it is not necessary to float a bond issue to apply the remedy," says Consumers Union in a special study. The *New York Times* agrees:

> The traffic problem in New York is of such magnitude and has been with us so long that the city's initiative has become almost numb in surrender to futility. The half-measures under way are largely routine responses prompted by a hopeless task. What is missing is a massive, centralized regional attack on the whole traffic-transportation problem.

THE URBAN FIELD

Congestion is less serious in the suburbs, and the air is somewhat better, but the trend is far from happy. The Committee on the Second Regional Plan for New York has described the curve as "a sweeping expansion of urbanization but a decrease in urbanity." Here are the major items:

> A search for country living by New Yorkers, which succeeds only until the next subdivision is bulldozed in
> A lengthening average trip to work, with a declining choice of accessible jobs
> Lengthening travel to recreation areas and other nonwork activities
> More cars and more traffic jams along Main Street
> Neighborhood patterns which inhibit neighborliness and the sense of belonging to a specific community
> A great exodus from the city, with little effort to retain the virtues of city living while overcoming its handicaps
> An exodus which leaves behind only those who cannot escape, or who have a high tolerance for the city's deficiencies
> A growing separation of Negro from white; of poor from affluent
> A growing problem for old people
> An increase in taxes multiplied by the crazy-quilt pattern of unplanned expansion
> A growing ugliness, the Regional Committee concludes, over the whole urban field

The New York region now has 1,500 political units with taxing power, including the town I live in. Attempts to consolidate these units, and to introduce some order into the region as a whole, are met by bitter opposition from local residents and politicians, especially in all-white suburbs. Yet the people in the New York urban field, city and suburbs together, have a common stake in the area's economy, its transport, water supply, sewage and refuse disposal, smog, crime, open space and recreation: a common stake, that is, in its livability.

The *New York Times* records the ruin of the remaining open spaces in the borough of Staten Island:

> The bulldozers are, every day, destroying wooded hills as matchstick houses march ruthlessly across fields and farms. . . . The community has failed to plan for predictable and pressing needs; it has guaranteed a future of disorder and squalor, a form of

municipal masochism that New York has developed to a high art.

A cartoon in *Life* in 1965 shows a huge truck loaded with skyscrapers, apartment houses, supermarkets, dumps, subdivisions, careening along with nobody at the wheel. There are 50 million people in the suburbs of American cities in 1967, with another 50 million predicted by the end of the century. At present rates of growth, 85 per cent of all Americans will then be living not necessarily downtown, but in the urban field— almost a complete reversal of the ratio between city and country since the Constitution was adopted in 1787.

In poll after poll Americans say they want a little house in the country with a garden. The urban field, however, simply does not permit a half-acre lot for every family. It might be possible in the Canadian tundra or Antarctica, but not around New York or St. Louis. The only way decently to house the population that is calculated for the end of the century is a combination of cluster zoning, garden apartments, and "new towns," which we will presently describe.

I live in an outlying area of the New York field, 60 miles from Times Square, in a town which has not yet become a "slurb." Our local Planning Commission, of which I am a member, is trying to maintain some sightliness and dignity in a comely old New England town, but the bulldozers are poised on every boundary. They have pretty well overrun the towns around us, and hungrily await new fields to conquer.

The distinguished architect, Victor Gruen, agrees that the automobile has demolished the nineteenth-century pattern of city and suburbs, a pattern which depended on public transport, particularly the trolley car.[5] We have been concentrating on the improvement of private living standards, he says, and neglecting the *public* environment. He tells of an Italian newly

[5] In symposium, *Who Designs America?* See Reading List.

arrived in Boston who said; "I bathe and dress better than I did in Naples, but then I don't know where to go." In Naples he went out to a public park with fountains and flowers; he sat beside his friends in a sidewalk café, with wine and good talk. In Boston he does not know where to go.

Gruen quotes Gertrude Stein, when she was interviewed about her impressions of the city of Oakland, California.

"How do you like it there?"

"There," she replied, "there is no there, there."

NOTE ON RIOTS

New York, Newark, Detroit, Los Angeles, and other American cities are suffering from a severe epidemic of rioting, with many dead and wounded, and whole sections looted and burned. The National Guard, and in some cases the Army, have been called in. The reasons for the riots are complicated, but one cause is sufficiently clear: technological change.

The mechanical cotton picker, the bulldozer, and other agricultural machines have been pushing Negroes off the land and into city slums. In the *New York Times* Bayard Rustin says that 500,000 Negroes a year have been leaving the cotton fields, while only 40,000 have been able to find their way into the suburbs. During World War II, when migration was high, there were plenty of jobs for the un-skilled in munitions plants. Now automation has sharply reduced factory jobs for the unskilled. To make matters worse, the factories, like the middle class, are moving out to the suburbs.

Negroes are thus up against low-wage work with no future in the service trades, or no jobs at all. A better formula for the frustration-aggression cycle would be hard to find. Many promises have been made by politicians—the Great Society, the War on Poverty—but very little has actually been ac-complished. "If a society," says Rustin, "is interested in stability, it should either not make promises, or it should keep them."

The trend shows the great city in America becoming a kind of black island, spreading like a giant ink blot—in the words of Victor Palmer—over the metropolitan core. "The Negro, the Puerto Rican, the Mexican, the poor and the aged, have missed the last train to suburbia."

AROUND THE WORLD

New York may be a prime exhibit in the trend toward urban decay, but it is not alone. All large American cities suffer from similar afflictions, and so do big cities around the world, including rich ones like London and poor ones like Calcutta—where 600,000 are said to sleep in the streets.

The chief troubles in affluent cities are the motorcar and alienation; in poor cities the chief trouble is peasants pouring in from the land where they can no longer make a living. They begin looking for a job and a home, but the jobs are limited, and housing is only in old slums, or in new shantytowns of corrugated iron. Five thousand migrants arrive in Rio every day, according to Charles Abrams, and 65 percent of the population of Caracas is composed of shantytown squatters. Abrams observes:

The day when the earth must hold seven billion is no futher away than World War I. The impact will be felt most in the cities of the less developed world. Although total population in these regions will grow by 40 percent in 15 years, urban population will double. . . . The human race is pouring into the cities at a pace which can only be called catastrophic.[6]

COUNTERTRENDS

One could go on interminably piling up evidence that Megalopolis is growing beyond the adaptability of human na-

[6] *Man's Struggle for Shelter*. MIT Press, 1964.

ture, and is fast becoming anti-city. No evidence is really needed in affluent societies beyond the wholesale migration of city-dwellers to the suburbs in search of living space. No evidence is needed for nonaffluent societies beyond photographs of the proliferating shantytowns, or of homeless thousands sleeping in the streets.

A number of countertrends are already discernible, some to be sure still on paper, others in solid construction. The major one is the dawning attempt to remove automobiles from all, or part, of the core city, thus relieving both traffic jams and air pollution. Parallel to this is the "new towns" movement, whereby brand new satellite communities are built around the core city as a check to urban sprawl. Let us look briefly at each.

ELIMINATING THE PRIVATE CAR

In San Francisco a system of mass transit called BART is under construction, to replace commuting by automobile. When it is ready, the cost to the commuter from suburb to core city is estimated at one-quarter of what he now pays for driving his own car—in solitary splendor and increasing nervous tension—to town. If BART proves successful, it will be widely emulated.

In Europe mass transit is further advanced. Munich, for instance, is building new subways and belt lines, while excluding most private vehicles from the central core. In Japan mass transit is proceeding at a fantastic pace. The technology of safe speeds at 100 miles an hour or more is building up. Compare this with the normal bumper-to-bumper parade at five miles an hour.

The automobile is also under legal attack and is actually banned from small sections of some cities. Pedestrian malls are being created in the center, where shoppers may wander among trees, flowers, and fountains without danger of extermination. In some of them you find small electric vehicles, traveling sedately with no poisonous exhausts. Perhaps they are the forerunners of the only kind of motorcar which will be permitted in the core city. An electric car powered by battery is noiseless, fumeless, and simple to operate and maintain. The unsolved technical problem is a better storage battery. When one is achieved, the motorist instead of stopping for gas would stop to leave the old battery for recharging and get a new light model installed.

The great auto makers of Detroit are hard at work on a nonpollution car. Ford is experimenting with a sodium-sulphur battery, General Motors with a fuel-cell prime mover. This technological innovation would generate electricity to power a motor directly from a chemical reaction. The fuel-cell may be the car of the future—little ones for city traffic, big ones for cross-country trips.

Here is a countertrend well worth watching—an individual motorcar which is cheaper, simpler, and more durable than the present type of car, and which leaves the air clean. If the United States should make a complete change to electric cars, it would add 500 billion kilowatt hours to the sales of electric power companies for recharging batteries. This is 50 percent of the present power output—and the utility companies, both private and public, are all agog! "Utilities Rooting for New Electric Cars," said a *New York Times* headline in 1966. On the other hand, the great oil companies are now taking full-page advertisements to oppose any such move. A battle of industrial giants is clearly on the trend curve—clean power versus petroleum.

NEW TOWNS

Here is Tapiola in Finland, a satellite of Helsinki, the capital.[7] It is a balanced community, built completely anew, with

[7] Wolf Von Eckardt in *Harper's Magazine,* December, 1965.

housing for all income levels, industry, shops, recreation areas, parks, and open space. Children walk to school, dodging no motorcars. Adults walk to their local work, if they do not commute to Helsinki. Yet space is provided for one car for every family. A miracle? No, just sound, intensive design for the motor age.[8]

Here is Reston, satellite of Washington, D.C. Ultimately it will house 75,000 people. Already many residents are living in handsome town houses beside its lake. It will serve all income levels with shops, light industry, theaters, schools, four golf courses, swimming pools, all the amenities. The motorcar will be allowed for, but kept strictly subservient to people. Robert Simon, a private builder, is behind this development. Wolf Von Eckardt argues for 350 new towns like Reston and Tapiola to surround American cities, housing ultimately 35 million people.

Mr. Gruen pushes the trend still further. He outlines a whole new structure for Megalopolis to replace the present horse-and-buggy gridiron. It consists of a series of "new towns," grouped into satellite cities, which in turn are grouped into a great core city. It provides for small face-to-face communities where you know your neighbors, inside these larger aggregates. The total population might be several million, but mass transport will take you to the airport from the Metrocenter in 17 minutes. The New York Second Regional Plan is also working on a series of satellite cities around New York.

All such proposals for sick cities—new towns, reconstructed old towns, mass transit, pollution engineering, pedestrian malls—have a vital connection with structural unemployment resulting from automation. What are blue-collar—yes, and white-collar—workers going to do when computers have taken away their work? (We shall examine this question at more length in Chapter 9.)

[8] Clarence Stein and others pioneered this trend in Radburn, a small community near New York, in the 1920's.

Well, here is a great deal for them to do in all categories, for many years to come. They can make the urban field habitable again, with Stockholm, Helsinki, Amsterdam, and Reston as guides. They can make it really beautiful as well as livable, including all modern improvements. A city where tranquilizers are in very short supply.

We can hardly grasp what technology could do for us if we really gave it a chance. It will take many billions of manhours, and even more billions of dollars, but the solid wealth created should justify the cost. One can envision a counter-trend for Megalopolis which goes far beyond current plans for urban renewal, a project financed jointly by government and giant corporations, to a total which, over the years, might rival—a daring analogy, I admit—half the gross national product for one year, say $400 billion for all American cities.

Let us now turn to the most cheerful major trend of technology—the promise of a cheap, and perhaps everlasting, supply of inanimate energy.

7

ENERGY

PERHAPS the best single index to measure the growth of technology is the use of inanimate energy. Some years ago I calculated that the U.S. used 40 horsepower for every man, woman, and child in the country. Now the figure has about doubled. I used to argue, too, that once poverty had been abolished, people could devote their attention to achieving the "good life" for all. Now, as the reports on juvenile delinquency come in from the affluent suburbs, I am not so sure.

Energy is the basis of civilization, and a direct cause of material prosperity. The first cities were built by human muscle, aided, in some areas, by animal power—oxen, horses, mules. The Indians of Peru had llamas, but the Maya of Mexico had no beast of burden at all. The pyramids of Egypt apparently were built by the Nile villagers in off seasons.

The original source of inanimate energy was of course firewood for cooking and heating caves. Then came wind for sails and windmills, and falling water for grinding grain. Coal did not amount to much until the industrial revolution, while petroleum as a fuel is only a century old. Big hydroelectric dams are still more recent, and nuclear power arrived only at the end of World War II. There has been some minor utilization of heat from the sun for power, and the fuel cell is in the offing, as we have seen.

Thirteen percent of all U.S. horsepower in 1850 came from human energy, according to one estimate. By 1900 the ratio had fallen to 5 percent, by 1950 to less than one percent. Animal power is not much in evidence in the United States today—horses and mules suffer from technological unemployment—and it is probable that close to 99 percent of all mechanical work is done by inanimate energy. It comes from oil wells, coal mines, hydro dams, and now there is an increasing amount of nuclear energy from uranium. This last source has been growing at a brisk exponential rate, with no S-curve in sight.

Nuclear power derives, of course, from the same discoveries in pure science which destroyed Hiroshima. But instead of blowing the world into "a radioactive hulk," it can blow us into a Utopia of material wealth if not of complete happiness. The quantum jump envisioned by Dr. Platt is pure moonshine without the atom to power it.

A STRIPPED PLANET?

Atomic power is coming in just as other sources of energy are beginning to run out, together with many natural resources. There is not enough horsepower in all the rivers of the world to supply the world's present need for energy. Oil may last a generation or two, coal a good deal longer; but with population doubling by the year 2000, the outlook for supplying the world indefinitely with conventional fuels is exceedingly dim. Experts have calculated that there is not enough available iron ore, bauxite, copper, lead, or other essential minerals to give the world's present population the material goods which the average American family *now* enjoys. Meanwhile, too, the supply of fresh water is giving out in many areas, as we have seen.

Some gloomy prophets look for the final exhaustion of natural resources within a century or so—see, for instance,

George Darwin's book *The Next Million Years*.[1] Coal, iron, copper, and the rest will become more costly as the veins run thinner and deeper. These forecasters hold that as the number of people increases, resources per capita will decrease, until life on a stripped planet is thrust back to primitive agriculture, with the muscles of men and animals as the chief prime movers.

The probabilities, however, are strongly against any such trend. For a long time to come, new resources are likely to be developed more rapidly than old resources decline—always assuming that we keep out of nuclear wars. Energy is the most critical resource. As conventional fuels become more scarce and costly, energy from the atom promises to grow cheaper. At some point the curves will cross, and nuclear power will become dominant. This point is close at hand in the late 1960's. Furthermore, as we will demonstrate shortly, low-cost nuclear power can make increasingly available the resources which are now declining. The prospect of a stripped planet does not seem to be anywhere on the trend curve.

ATOMIC FUSION

The two processes for developing atomic power are quite different, and it is important to be clear about them. They are *fission*—which means splitting the atoms of a heavy element; and *fusion*—which means fusing or combining the atoms of a light element. Nuclear fusion was identified theoretically by physicists before fission, but its release in a practical power plant is still some years, perhaps decades, away. It results from fusing hydrogen atoms into helium, the next lightest element. Fission energy, on the contrary, is generated at the other end of the atomic scale, and is the result of *splitting* the heavy atoms of uranium and so generating a chain reaction.

Thorium, a heavy element, can also be split like uranium,

[1] Doubleday, 1952.

and so can plutonium, a man-made element not found in nature. Are there power possibilities in the 90 or so elements between? Perhaps, but scientists will have their hands full for quite a while with those at the extremes. When a nuclear explosion takes place, the light is said to be "brighter than a thousands suns"—blinding for life a man who is unfortunate enough to see it.

The fusion of hydrogen releases truly celestial energy, the transformation which actually takes place in the interior of our sun. What poet in his wildest imaginings would have dreamed of taming it here on earth? Yet scientists are determined to accomplish just this, and when they succeed, as they expect to, the world's energy problem should be forever solved. Fusion leaves no poisonous radioactivity as does fission, only the "clean ash of helium." This is one great advantage; the other is the source from which it will come. That source is sea water—all the oceans of the world. It has been calculated that they contain 100 quadrillion tons of hydrogen, enough to keep the fusion process going as far as we can glimpse the future.

It is exceedingly difficult, however, to control the fusing of hydrogen into helium, because of the enormous temperatures and pressures involved. The thermonuclear bomb is a fusion process, but to make it hot enough to detonate requires a small fission bomb in tandem. Both varieties are in the warhead. Laboratory men in the United States, Britain, and Russia are working on fusion, and are cautiously hopeful. Some scientists see a practical power plant in 10 years, some in 50 years; few believe it cannot be done. When we remember what the Manhattan Project did in a four-year crash program, we also can be cautiously optimistic.

R. F. Post, writing in the *Scientific American* for December, 1966, sees the problem of fusion "slowly yielding." Data are out in the open and freely exchanged around the world's laboratories—a great help in any R & D. The prime problem is how to generate enough heat and keep it stable. The central event is "plasma," controlled probably by a magnetic field. The outline of the problem is taking firm shape, says Dr. Post. "We have little doubt that the dream of extracting unlimited energy from the seas will one day become a reality."

The head of Fusion Research for the U.S. Atomic Energy Commission, Dr. A. S. Bishop, has no doubts about the raw material supply in the oceans' hydrogen. "There is enough," he says, "to supply the earth with energy at a thousand times the current rate of consumption for 20 million years." Maybe we will not have to take off for Neptune.

ATOMIC FISSION

Energy derived from fission, the splitting of heavy atoms in a chain reaction, is already in operation in power plants a good deal smaller than the fusion process will probably call for. It involves two serious problems, however: what disposition can be made of the dangerous radioactive wastes resulting from the reaction? And second, how long will uranium ore last? The reaction depends on a buried mineral, just as conventional power depends on coal and oil. Uranium in the earth may, or may not, last longer than coal, but certainly there are no deposits to compare with 100 quadrillion tons of hydrogen in the oceans.

The cost of building a nuclear power plant is much greater than that of a conventional plant for an equal kw output. Once built, however, the cost of fuel year by year is much less, especially the cost of transporting it. Admiral Hyman Rickover, who developed the atomic submarine, is working on what he calls a "seed-blanket" atomic reactor, which will further reduce the fuel cost. It will use thorium as the major fuel, and might run for as much as nine years on a single charge. Rickover says that reactors of this type could extend fuel resources by several hundred years. "We are not dealing with peanuts here," he says. "We are dealing with the future welfare of this country and perhaps of the whole world. You can't conduct a society without electrical energy."[2]

A neat confirmation of the Admiral's last remark came in the 1965 power failure which paralyzed New York, as described earlier. Subways, railways, elevators, air traffic, refrigeration, heat, light, traffic lights, TV and radio—all vanished. If power had not been restored within hours, New York would have had to be abandoned—a consummation which not everybody would deplore.

There is brisk competition among Western manufacturers bidding for reactors to be built in India, Japan, Italy, Spain, Holland, and Switzerland. Soviet Russia is building reactors in East Germany, Hungary, Bulgaria, Czechoslovakia. The General Electric Company reports that costs per kilowatt have been reduced 50 percent from 1961 to 1966, and will be reduced further. Meanwhile the search for the new uranium deposits is being briskly stepped up.

The boldest program, as I write, is the $500 million joint government-private (mixed economy) plant for the Los Angeles area, "geared to the simultaneous production of power, and desalted sea water, at a rate of 150 million gallons a day at a cost of 20 cents per 1,000 gallons compared with current desalting costs of around a dollar."[3] Commissioner James T. Ramey of the Tennessee Valley Authority looks to costs reduced to 8 cents before long. At this figure, a chain of nuclear energy centers, he says, producing power, fertilizers, and other chemicals as well, might go far to break the vicious poverty cycle in the Hungry World.

NUCLEAR WASTES

The toughest problem in fission power has been the disposal of radioactive wastes, which pollute land and water. Flushed

[2] Before Joint Senate-House Atomic Committee, March 18, 1965.
[3] New York Times, May 26, 1967.

into rivers, or sealed in concrete containers and dumped into caves or ocean deeps, their terminal effects are still uncertain, but could be very serious.

A conference in Vienna in 1966, called by the International Atomic Energy Agency and reported by Walter Sullivan of the *New York Times,* discussed this problem and concluded that the threat has not yet reached the lethal level. At the conference was Dr. R. F. Foster, who could hardly bear to look at a whitefish. He had been eating them steadily for years in the interests of science. They were caught in the Columbia River below the large atomic installations at Hanford, Washington. Dr. Foster probably carries the heaviest load of radioactive zinc of any man alive. Tests show, however, that the "hot zinc" now inside him is less than 10 percent of the amount considered permissible for human consumption.

Other scientists at Vienna reported on the eating of "laver bread," a delicacy derived from seaweed exposed to nuclear wastes. They reported on the effect of phosphorus 32 in rivers, and on strontium 90 flushed out from the Oak Ridge atomic plant in Tennessee. The upshot of many learned papers, according to Sullivan, seems to have been that radioactive wastes discharged into rivers and seas "are actually declining because of improved processing techniques."

Well, that's fine. But what will the scientists report at their conferences when the energy generated from fission doubles, triples, and quadruples? The layman will feel better when he is sure that fusion power will come successfully out of the laboratory, with no hot zinc for the insides of courageous professors, no hazard to uranium miners, and no question of exhausting the supply.

EFFECTS ON MEGALOPOLIS

Energy from fusion will probably require large plants, but energy from fission can be generated in small plants located

wherever you please. Thus nuclear power can be more
widely distributed than conventional power. Could this slow
the present mass migration to Megalopolis? It will no longer
be necessary to put industry near the fuel source as in the
past—say, Pittsburgh or the Ruhr. Fuel can be taken to industry anywhere—in the Chilean copper belt, the Australian
desert, Antarctica, Central Asia, Japan. Nuclear fuel is about
one million times as concentrated as conventional fuels, and,
on the breeder principle, a single fueling may last for many
years.

J. Bronowski, the well-known British scientist, pictures a
small nuclear plant forming the heart of a community in the
country, a town of perhaps 30,000. Such a town can be as
well equipped with facilities for modern living as the largest
city. "It is not necessary to retreat from the disaster of Megalopolis," he says, "into the inertia of the rural village."[4] This
development can put a "new town" into a completely rural
setting, surrounded by a greenbelt of woods and meadows, no
longer a satellite of the core city. Thus atomic power, with its
small outlay for the transportation of fuel, makes living space
more flexible.

Atomic power, too, may make big power dams obsolete,
especially in the American West. Donaldson Koons, a geolo-
gist who has spent some 25 years mapping in and around the
Grand Canyon of the Colorado, brings an indictment of two
proposed dams which has nothing to do with scenic destruction. He says that the dams will certainly produce cheap
power, but at the same time they will tend to dry up further
the whole Southwest region, which is already very dry. They
will cause the loss of half a million acre-feet of water a year by
evaporation. "A few more projects of this sort," he says, "and
there won't be any Colorado River." In the humid East reservoirs do not seriously upset the balance of nature by evapora-

[4] *New York Times Magazine,* July 15, 1962.

tion; in the dry West "they can be a disaster."

It would seem that atomic power is the ideal alternative. It will save the flow of the river, save the scenery, save the hydrologic cycle, while also producing kilowatts at a very low cost.

FRESH WATER FROM THE SEA

A nuclear power plant can also desalt sea water for the beleaguered crop lands of Arizona, or anywhere else.

The long water crisis in New York has brought forth at least one cosmic proposal. Why not, it is asked, turn Long Island Sound into a fresh-water sea, fed by the depolluted Hudson and Connecticut rivers? The Zuider Zee in the Netherlands is a model. One virtue of this proposal is that it first demands the cleaning up of two despoiled rivers. But if New Yorkers really want fresh water, at a far more reasonable cost, a series of desalting plants could forever forestall another water crisis. The United States Atomic Energy Commission is recommending a giant nuclear plant for the New Jersey–New York City area. It will not only produce 300 million gallons of fresh water every day, but also generate huge blocks of electric power. It could be used on a stand-by basis, to supplement the present system of upstate reservoirs, or as an alternative, four such plants, producing 1.2 billion gallons a day, could be the main supply for the whole New York urban field.

The United States and Russia have signed a formal agreement to exchange desalting technology, and the U.S. is helping Israel to build a large nuclear plant on the Mediterranean coast. Similar projects are under discussion for Egypt, Tunisia, and Mexico. Russia is contructing a huge plant on the Caspian Sea. The boom is on throughout the world.

Let us pause a moment and note an effect broader than just fresh water. These plants are going to *enlarge living space,* a countertrend to the shrinkages detailed in Chapter 5. Not only can they prevent present areas, like Arizona, from drying up, but they can restore to livability certain deserts, caused by overgrazing or overlumbering in the historic past, in North Africa, for instance.

MINERALS

Nuclear energy will produce torrents of fresh water, and at the same time perform electrolysis on the salt residue and recover magnesium, copper, lead, and other valuable minerals. It can be used to grind up common rocks, such as granite, and recover the iron, tungsten, and uranium which the rocks contain, at a reasonable cost. It should also be helpful in processing oil shales for petroleum.

Cheap energy can be used to mine the earth's mantle, where huge deposits of minerals are buried. Operation Mohole, designed to drill through the ocean floor, is the beginning of such an operation. New techniques are also under development for exploiting very deep mines if adequate energy is available. Automatic machines can do the work in temperatures no human being could endure.

Sea water contains relatively little iron to be reclaimed by electrolysis, but research in space points to a possible supply. Certain large asteroids now orbiting the sun are almost pure iron. Arthur C. Clarke, in his book *Profiles of the Future*,[5] suggests that they be captured and stocked near the steel mills—a project obviously requiring close international cooperation. Some dreamy fellows even hope to mine the moon for minerals—but they do not explain how the ore is to be transported back to earth. Mr. Clarke wisely discounts the moon, but he offers a number of stimulating, and to me practical, ideas for salvaging natural resources. He sums them up with a very practical warning: "In this inconceivably enormous universe we can never run out of energy or matter. But we can all too easily run out of brains."

[5] See Reading List.

The final solution to raw materials which are growing scarce, and one a good deal more realistic than mining the moon, is to *create them synthetically.* The Atomic Energy Commission already creates plutonium, an element not found in nature. The age-long dream of the alchemists of transmuting base metals into gold is no longer purely in the realm of science fiction. It can be done theoretically, but requires a lot of energy, a kind of $E = mc^2$ in reverse. Atomic building blocks can be extracted from common materials, such as sand or stone, and, with abundant energy, fashioned into any element or compound we desire, "from diamonds to vitamins," Bronowski says. This will not happen tomorrow, but it is on the trend curve. The vast development of plastics, led by Bakelite, is a forerunner of the trend.

SUNLIGHT

Gerard Piel, publisher of the *Scientific American,* calculates that a third of all U.S. energy is now utilized to heat houses, office buildings, stores, and factories, while a quarter of all electric power goes to light them. New discoveries in solid-state physics—of which the transistor is the best-known example—may make it possible, he says, for the sun to do much of this heating and lighting. The transistor also can help a solar battery convert sunlight directly into electricity. Piel believes that solid-state physics will make an electric automobile practical, and thus reduce air pollution, as noted in Chapter 6.

WEALTH UNLIMITED

By this time it should be clear that inanimate energy is our grandest form of material wealth. Failing it, we should presently be thrust back into the Stone Age. But if energy is abundant and cheap, a material Utopia is not an impossible dream. If my discourse occasionally sounds like Sunday supplement science, I cannot help it. Nothing is predicted in these pages without a firm grounding in sober research, while power from the atom, and the desalting of sea water, among others, are well along in the development stage of R & D. *The knowledge is available;* all we need are the brains to apply it wisely.

Let us end the chapter with a categorical list of what we can reasonably expect from nuclear energy, directed to peaceful purposes and intelligently managed.

1. It can industrialize the low-energy world, two-thirds of mankind, and virtually equalize living standards everywhere. Poverty could be obliterated—provided, of course, that population control goes along with it.

2. It can help to reduce economic rivalries between nations by making abundant resources available to all. The struggle for scarce materials will be muted; every nation will be a Have nation. Belligerent nationalism will also be undermined by the necessity of joint action in drilling through the earth's crust, capturing ferric satellites, exploiting the seas and Antarctica.

3. Nuclear energy will make it possible to put cities, towns, and communities anywhere on the map, and facilitate a more flexible distribution of population.

4. It can solve much of the fresh-water shortage which is now threatening us, and even irrigate and reclaim deserts. If water is to be pumped a reasonable distance inland, the same plant which desalts the sea water can furnish power for the job.

5. It will be invaluable for the rebuilding of Megalopolis, a project demanding, as we have seen, great blocks of both inanimate and human energy.

6. It will give industry lower costs for power, and thus help pay for necessary antipollution installations.

7. It will make practical the exploitation of minerals now buried in the earth's crust and at sea bottom.

8. It will make practical the reclaiming of minerals by

grinding up common rocks and by applying electrolysis to ocean salts.

9. At some point on the trend curve, energy will be abundant enough to synthesize any element we desire. I doubt if we will desire gold—except a little for dentistry and medicine.

With any luck—and considerable intelligence, to be sure— we have in the splitting of uranium and the fusing of hydrogen a solvent for most of mankind's physical problems. This is technology's greatest contribution to human welfare. It should be helpful in psychological problems as well.

When various other trends outlined in this book induce an atmosphere of gloom, let us not forget the reactors now, at this moment, going into their concrete pits in power plants around the world, and the easing of national rivalries and tensions which are a logical result.

8

THE MIXED ECONOMY

WHEN a society has less than one percent of its physical work done by human muscle, receives very little from draft animals, and obtains up to 99 percent from coal, oil, gas, hydros, and now the atom, it is obvious that inanimate energy is the prime factor in the creation of that society's wealth. Energy and technology already have had an accelerating impact on the economy, both physically and ideologically. Indeed, all high-energy societies are moving toward a so-called mixed economy, a "mix" in which both private and public sectors are recognized as essential, and are encouraged to supplement one another for maximum production. Thus in the United States the private sector manufactures the cars, and the public sector provides the roads for the cars to run on. Government is also beginning to regulate the design of the car, in the interest of safety and cleaner air. Again, the private sector manufactures the television sets, and the public sector controls the airwaves —at least in theory. There is also a third sector, privately owned but not operated for profit, like universities and foundations.

The trend toward a mixed economy is massive not only in the United States, but within its well-advertised antagonist, Russia. It moves, however, from opposite poles. In the United States the public sector is expanding; in the U.S.S.R. it is shrinking, especially in centralized planning for local enterprises. Both effects come from similar technological pressures; both are slowed by ideological rigidity. "Government interference," which we have considered morally wrong, for instance, the Russians have considered morally normal; they disapprove of *private* enterprise.

All open societies—the countries of Western Europe, Australia, New Zealand, Canada, Japan—are moving along with the United States in the direction of a mixed economy, some of them much more rapidly than the United States. At the same time the various satellite states of Russia, together with independent Yugoslavia, are doing likewise. The terms "capitalism" and "Communism" are making less and less sense as descriptive of what is actually going on. Technology demands economic interdependence, assembly line production, vast power grids, management techniques which are standard in high-energy societies everywhere.

FROM RICARDO TO KEYNES TO GALBRAITH

The United States has lived through two periods of economic theory and is now entering a third. As technical and industrial developments have changed our economic behavior, the interpretation of that behavior must also change, though interpretation usually follows at some distance behind the tangible events. Witness how gold is still important in economic thinking, and unimportant in tangible behavior. How long is it since the reader has used a gold coin in an actual transaction? Gold is prized by speculators, but has ceased to be a useful base for money.

The three periods of economic theory in the United States are the classical, whose chief theoretician was David Ricardo; the Keynesian, whose expounder was John Maynard Keynes; and now the surprising beginnings of the mixed or balanced economy, first outlined in depth by John Kenneth Galbraith in his book, *The Affluent Society.*

In the pioneering days of America, everybody had to work hard so that there might be enough to eat. Now, in our affluent condition, as Professor Benjamin Graham suggests, everybody has to eat hard so that there may be enough work. If consumers relax their efforts, unemployment looms. The Puritan ethic of hard work and thrift is still strong in the American belief system, but sometimes difficult to find in the market place— an excellent example of cultural lag.

The classical economists assumed that the system if let alone—*laissez faire* they called it—would always find its equilibrium in full employment. Wages, they said, and prices, and interest rates, responding to market demand, would automatically bring about this happy condition. An "invisible hand," they said, kept the economy steady. Any artificial raising of wages by labor unions, or fixing of prices by business men, or manipulating of interest rates by central banks, would destroy the harmony of *laissez faire,* and cause unemployment and depression.

The classical theory had some relevance in the early nineteenth century, with its little ironmasters and shopkeepers. But with the rise of Big Business, and the expanding output made possible by new inventions, such as assembly line production, it became less relevant. In the Great Depression, following the stock market crash of 1929, classical theory lost all contact with reality. Attempts to let nature take her course, and sermons declaring that everything would be all right in 90 days, only made matters more serious. Mr. Hoover tried to follow the classical theory, with the most dismal results.

Governments were finally forced to intervene in all high-energy societies, lest mass starvation lead to revolution. When Mr. Roosevelt stood in the rain on the steps of the Capitol in Washington and said, "We have nothing to fear but fear itself," many citizens had ample grounds for fear and were suffering acute hardship. A quarter of the population once gainfully employed was on the streets, all the banks were closed, and money had ceased to function. No one who did not live through that dreadful spring of 1933 can begin to appreciate how close we came to utter disaster. Lines of destitute men and women shuffled around whole city blocks, awaiting bowls of soup; mothers picked over garbage dumps for scraps of food for their children; farmers got out their guns and shot sheriffs who tried to foreclose their mortgages.

From the vantage point of the 1960's we can realize the tragic paradox. Fifteen million unemployed citizens, from all former income levels, were desperately eager to go back to work. A magnificent industrial plant, including the latest in mass production, untouched by bombing raids, fire or flood, stood paralyzed with chimneys cold and wheels unturning. Its owners, though they were only too anxious for workers to return, were unable to rehire them, and often made the situation worse by further retrenchments. There were plenty of savings, but few dared to invest them.

One has to be blinded by a rigid ideology indeed not to see the tragedy of this impasse. Somebody had to act as a catalyst and connect the idle men with the idle plants. Somebody had to start the idle money moving. This was the historic role of Franklin Roosevelt and his New Deal. The wheels began to turn, but slowly. The role of the government was distrusted by nearly all business leaders; the function of a compensatory economy, as demonstrated by Keynes, was practically unknown. The Depression abated somewhat, but lingered on until the Japanese attack on Pearl Harbor in 1941.

The two major concerns of the classical economists were how to increase production and how to distribute the output with some justice. The first has become minor in an economy of abundance, a condition where technology increases output so lavishly that demand from consumers must be artificially stimulated, to the point of producing annual models without any particular function except new styling. Mass production makes no sense without mass consumption; we have to "eat hard" to keep up with the output of Kansas farms and the assembly lines of Detroit.

Today in the United States more than 60 percent of all families are in the affluent class, their eyes steadily fixed on two cars, a plastic swimming pool, TV in full color, and a second house for week ends. But nearly 20 percent of all Americans are still poor, in city slums and such rural regions as Appalachia. The measuring scale has shifted, however, and their need, distressing as it is, shows the smallest ratio of poor people ever known in a civilized society. The remaining families are on the border line, neither poor nor affluent. In sharp contrast with 1933, though many suffer from malnutrition, nobody in America today is actually starving.

KEYNES AND THE "NEW ECONOMICS"

Classical theory could not account for the Great Depression in any helpful way; indeed, its principles of thrift and abstinence had seriously retarded recovery. Technology had abolished the little ironmaster and the self-sufficient farmer, and there was no retreat to Ricardo's world of the 1830's, or even to President McKinley's world of 1900. Where was a theory which ran closer to the facts? Keynes, in his tough, difficult book *The General Theory of Employment, Interest and Money,* published in 1936, provided such a thesis. It deeply shocked the classicists, but gradually government and even professional economists surrendered to its logic.

Keynes argued that there was no invisible hand, no assurance that *laissez faire,* or leaving things alone, would sooner or later guarantee full employment. He emphasized what surely would bring full employment, namely, total monetary *demand.* Reducing wages—as sternly advocated in the Depression—would only *reduce* demand for goods and services —it would, he said, only balance the budget at naught on both sides.

Following this analysis came the remedy: *Keep total demand at a level to provide full employment.* If necessary, said Keynes, supplement private spending with public spending, as both contribute to demand. Do this whenever the "propensity to save" exceeds the "propensity to invest." Make idle money circulate and go to work. If public spending is called for, do *not* increase taxes to cover the outlay, for this will reduce private spending by taxpayers, and lessen total demand. Do not be afraid of deficit financing. An unbalanced budget is infinitely preferable to a major depression.

Per contra, said Keynes, if the economy begins to overheat, check inflation by increasing taxes or reducing public expenditures, or both. This reduces total demand and steadies prices. Never mind balancing the national budget every year; balance the whole economy by keeping demand at par, and the budget will take care of itself.

This is the essence of the "compensatory economy" recommended by Keynes. Spend when a depression threatens, retrench when inflation threatens.

The open societies of Europe adopted the formula in varying degrees after World War II. President Eisenhower abhorred the idea of deficit spending, but his government practiced it in a generous way during the 1950's, without disaster. Indeed, the national debt rose more slowly than population, and thus debt per capita actually declined.

Both Presidents Kennedy and Johnson continued the Keynesian formula, which has now become almost a new orthodoxy. A dramatic confirmation was found in the 1964 income tax cut, which, when the books were balanced, showed an actual *reduction* in the federal deficit, precisely as Keynes predicted. Lower tax rates encouraged more spending by taxpayers, which in turn stimulated market demand, and thus generated more government revenue from taxes, despite the lower rates.

The remaining advocates of *laissez faire,* apparently unable to grasp this sequence, protested that it must have been done with mirrors. To get more tax revenues by reducing tax rates does, we must admit, require a little concentrated thought. As the United States economy began to quicken with the large public spending for war in Vietnam, many economists, following Keynes, called for an *increase* in income taxes. This would of course reduce private spending and with it total demand, thus checking inflation. It was not done, and prices rose in 1966.

The key statistic in the whole operation is a count of the unemployed. A reliable count used to be impossible, but modern sampling theory has now made it reasonably accurate. It is necessary to spend enough so that the rate of unemployed workers does not go much above *3 percent*[1] of the labor force, which allows for workers moving from job to job. If private spending does not suffice, let public spending fill the gap.

Observe how far this formula is from the theory of orthodox socialism. Only fiscal (tax rate) and monetary (interest rate) controls are involved, plus accurate statistics. Socialism, as you know, calls for the "public ownership of the principal means of production"—lands, factories, transport, and the rest. The Keynesian formula calls for no transfer of ownership to the state; production remains largely in private hands. The government adjusts tax rates and interest rates, and spends more or spends less, depending on the count of the unemployed. It spends for defense, for social security, public health, conservation—outlays which are seldom subject to profitable

---

[1] Some economists prefer a standard of 2 percent.

operation on the market. It would be difficult to package the Hoover Dam, or a Polaris submarine, or Medicare, on the shelves of even the grandest supermarket. Ignoring this cardinal distinction, ultraconservatives continue to call Lord Keynes a Communist—or a Fabian socialist, which in their book is even worse. They suffer from the romantic notion that only private money-making creates wealth.

BEYOND KEYNES

All right. An open society, such as the United States, or Sweden, or Japan, follows the Keynesian formula. It keeps its gross national product increasing a bit faster than population, while the unemployment rate is held down by the compensatory measures just described. There may be minor swings in either direction, but a government which has accurate statistics and knows its Keynes, can see a swing coming well in advance, and take steps to moderate it. There need never be another Great Depression, never a runaway inflation. It would be rash to hold that governments in all open societies have their hands quite so firmly on the economic levers, but the techniques are there for them to use.

So we need not await the full development of atomic energy; an economic Utopia is practically here? Alas, it is not. We need only look at the trends recorded in the last few chapters to see how far from Utopia is even the most astute society today. Regard America: its GNP is close to three-quarters of a trillion dollars a year, unemployment is less than 4 percent, the roads are full of new cars, the marinas full of new cabin cruisers, the backyards full of plastic swimming pools. Statistically and gadget-wise we are terrific! But so far as a solid foundation for the good life is concerned, we are in a mess. The pollution of our air, the fouling of our waters, the crime rate, slums, race riots, and urban sprawl are all going right along up with the GNP.

Keynes's theory is working, to be sure, but again events are outrunning it, while the economic doctors hesitate to prescribe remedies not in the pharmacopoeia. A growing number of students, led by Galbraith, are trying to update the formulas. In *The Affluent Society* Galbraith contends that there is a disproportionate allocation of resources between private spending and public needs, between "private opulence and public squalor." He draws an unforgettable picture of an opulent family, descending from its sleek, air-conditioned car, with a refrigerated lunch hamper, to picnic beside a polluted stream lined with empty beer cans.

Dollar totals are not good enough. Unless public needs, especially the maintenance of living space, are adequately provided for, we cannot enjoy our private opulence, except in snatches. Furthermore the snatches are decreasing. What good is a private automobile without adequate public roads, parking space, and traffic controls? What enjoyment can one have in even the most luxurious New York penthouse if the water supply fails or the electric power goes off? Who wants to stay in the most glamorous resort town if the air is tainted day and night with rank odors from a polluted bay? Economic growth and high employment certainly define a condition preliminary to solving many social problems. But problems remain which cannot be solved by dollar growth, while new problems arise as the direct result of affluence—such as the wastes recorded in earlier chapters.

The progression from the Keynesian standard of high demand and high employment to the more human goal of civilized living in a healthy environment will not be easy. There are many embattled pressure groups to be persuaded or overcome. Consider those real estate interests which have a stake in slums and slurbs. Consider the industries which have a vested interest in pollution. Consider the imposing billboard lobby. Or consider those fellow citizens in California who picketed to continue the destruction of a lordly redwood forest, because they were dependent on the lumber company for their jobs.

My wife once asked me, referring to a well-known real estate operator, "Who has done more to make New York uninhabitable?" The list of candidates, from heroin peddlers to the builders of the Pan Am Building, blocking mid-town Manhattan, is a formidable one. The *New York Times* in a leading editorial calls for an era beyond Keynes:

> Prosperity is not enough. Private spending cannot clear the smoggy air, clean the polluted rivers or abolish the hideous slums. More money in private pockets cannot teach a child, police a dark street, or enable an overworked doctor to be in two places at once. If the national purpose of a just, compassionate and truly free society is to be achieved, the President and Congress must see to it that the public needs of the national community are fully met. They are not being met now.

THE MIX INCREASES

In simplest terms a mixed economy is one where at least three sectors of economic activity are used impartially to do for the whole community those things which must be done to keep it livable. They are, again in simplest terms:

1. The private enterprise sector, organized for profit.
2. The public sector, not normally organized for profit, including all levels of government.
3. The private sector, furnishing goods and services which are *not* for profit. This rapidly growing field in the United States is usually overlooked when economic theory is discussed. It includes cooperative enterprises, churches, charities, universities, foundations, hospitals, clubs, fraternities, mutual insurance companies, savings and loan associations, trade unions, museums and libraries, and so on, a long list. In many cases, this sector tries to compensate for public squalor.

Various rough calculations show that the "mix" in the United States runs about 75 percent private in terms of manpower, including the nonprofit sector, and 25 percent public, including federal, state, and local governments. The actual mix, however, has now become so complex that any attempt to make a clean-cut division between public and private enterprises is very difficult. Eli Ginzberg, in his book, *The Pluralistic Economy,* points out that in the private-profit sector are most public utilities, including railroads, canals, water companies, gas, power, subways, telephone, banking, insurance. They are operated for profit but regulated by the government. We have already mentioned the private manufacture of automobiles, which are useless without public roads to run on. A more recent, and an even more complicated mix is nuclear power. The research which made it possible was strictly nonprofit, conducted by universities and government. In 1954, however, the Atomic Energy Commission opened up some of its data to private companies, including public utilities like Consolidated Edison. These companies hoped to make a profit from the sale of nuclear power, but a profit strictly regulated by government.

Still more intertwined is the relationship between the federal government and the defense industries, a $60-billion-a-year complex which President Eisenhower warned against in his farewell address. Says Ginzberg of this cat's cradle:

The Armed Forces have always relied on purchases in the market-place both for consumables and weapons. During the last two decades, however, there has been a radical alteration in the pattern. A considerable number of companies, some with annual sales of as much as $2 billion, sell almost all of their output to the Department of Defense. What they produce, the time allowed for production, the detailed specifications of quality, as well as the prices charged, and the profits that may be retained, are all determined by negotiation between the government and the company.

In many instances, the facilities used, and much of the know-how, have been provided by the government.

Here is a mix to end all mixes! What is private and what is public? We must also remember that the federal government is subsidizing many private universities with large research grants, and is underwriting various private industries, such as the merchant marine. Government also subsidizes the trucking industry by building the highways for the trucks to run on, to the despair of the railroad industry. Mr. Ginsberg calculates that more people are now directly employed in government (i.e., on the payroll) than in farming, mining, and construction combined. When the Republic was founded, we remember, over 90 percent of all the gainfully employed were farmers.

The mix, you see, is making a shambles of both capitalist and socialist ideologies, with their two-valued confrontation of public and private enterprise. Whatever the next decade may bring—short of an atomic war—the mixed economy will continue to expand and further dissolve the old slogans and the old textbooks.

THE GALBRAITH MODEL

Professor Galbraith in his book *The New Industrial State* offers a lively analysis of the mixed economy that exists in America today, and describes the probable dominant trend it will follow. Capitalism, he says, is evolving into a new industrial structure, closely tied to the state, where over-all planning, spurred by continuous technological innovation, is superseding the market economy of the classicists. It is downgrading the investment banker by getting the bulk of new capital from reinvested earnings, and is also undermining the old positions of the stockholder, the entrepreneur, and the labor union. The unions are not fought frontally so much as gradually deprived of their functions by automation.

The planning is conducted by 500 "mature" corporations

in the United States, which are in substantial control of electric power, oil, transport, communication, manufacturing and mining, entertainment, and a large share of retailing. The outmoded free market still operates for farmers and for merchants along Main Street, but the "System" no longer tolerates the uncertainties and instabilities of *laissez faire*. Modern industry measures its success by "its capacity to increase production in response to wants of its own creation."

The great firms are run in fact, if not in organization charts, says Galbraith, by technical specialists, who pay little attention to stockholders beyond assuring them of their conventional dividend, and not much more to the board of directors, whose members are mostly innocent of modern technology. The old captains of industry—the Morgans, the Garys, the Insulls, and the Fords—are fading from the scene.

The System is no longer interested in taking all the traffic will bear, but rather in keeping the traffic well heeled and healthy so that it can continue to absorb the System's massive output. To persuade the consumer to buy ever more sport cars, swimming pools, second houses, power mowers, air-conditioners, and colored television sets is a major goal of the System, and the persuasive specialists of Madison Avenue provide able assistance toward this goal. Leisure, contemplation, satisfaction with what one has, are not to be tolerated. Steady growth, both in the output of the firm and in gross national product, is mandatory, for the stability of the System depends thereon.

To achieve this goal, it is essential to forge a close working association with the government, be it controlled by Democrats or by Republicans. The logic is persuasive, and Galbraith is not the only competent observer to document it. The System needs customers with ample purchasing power. No one firm can guarantee that, but the state by insuring *aggregate demand* can guarantee it.

This is exactly what the federal government has been accomplishing through fiscal and monetary controls, running back to the days of the New Deal. It has set up strong defenses against both severe depression and runaway inflation. The state also provides vast programs of R & D ($16 billion in 1966), which are most helpful to business; it trains and educates specialists for the System's staff. Above all, the state cooperates with industry in producing the hardware and supplies for the military establishment, for the space program, for the Atomic Energy Commission, and for other huge technical operations where "the line between public and private authority is indistinct and in large measure imaginary. . . . When this is perceived, the central trends in American economic life become clear. On few matters is an effort to free the mind more rewarding." The Main Street merchant may continue to denounce government interference with some sincerity, but General Motors knows better.

The System is carrying the "mix" deeper and deeper into the American economy, but the effect on our citizenry leaves a good deal to be desired. The nonaffluent sector of the population lies outside the System, and so do measures to conserve and protect the environment. The System thrives on air pollution, traffic jams and Olympian piles of refuse. Indeed, the more stuff thrown away half-used, the better the growth in aggregate demand.

Looking into the future, Galbraith expects the "educational and scientific estate," whose members now operate the industrial system, to become increasingly restless and increasingly sensitive to the public welfare. These specialists already possess latent power, and if they should produce the political leadership, they might adjust the System's goals to include rescuing the poor and the environment. There is plenty of high technology available to create something close to that "near Paradise" glimpsed by the *New York Times* as the alternative to nuclear incineration.

One recalls the technocrats of Veblen, and the "open conspirators" of H. G. Wells. How is a runaway technology to be brought to heel except by those sufficiently educated to understand it? Or are the machines themselves dictating their imperatives to the engineers, as the gloomy prophets have predicted?

Whatever the caveats, as Galbraith so thoroughly documents, there is a powerful trend toward a mixed economy in America, and it strikingly differs from the standard concepts of either capitalism or socialism.

THE MIXED ECONOMY IN RUSSIA

While open societies are moving—or, better, being pushed —into an increasingly complicated mix of economic functions, the technological imperative is also pushing closed societies toward a similar mix. While classicists and ultraconservatives denounce "government interference" in the United States, hard-shell Marxists denounce the emergence of the profit motive in Russia.

Central state planning (the Gosplan) in Russia, dominant under Stalin, relaxed a little under Khrushchev, and has now surrendered to various techniques for more efficient production, techniques found in the private sector of open societies. Premier Kosygin, in an epoch-making speech in September, 1965, demanded the following reforms:

> Local plant managers must be given more power to hire and fire.
> They must be given more responsibility in procuring raw materials.
> They must be given more opportunity to make a profit and to invest it in the business.
> The Gosplan in Moscow must cease making detailed plans for local enterprises.

"These are immense innovations in the industrial structure of the Soviets," observed John Scott on his return from a recent visit in Russia. They make the plant manager, he says, something like a divisional manager in a large United States corporation. The latter runs his own shop except for changes in product and major capital outlays.

Mr. Scott is a seasoned reporter, commissioned by the publisher of *Time* to travel abroad and inspect economic conditions in various countries. He is fluent in five languages, and is particularly qualified to report on Russia, where he has lived and worked. Though he is impressed with the increase in industrial efficiency since the Stalin era (when he was employed in a steel mill in Magnitogorsk), and with the improvement in general living conditions, he has little use for the Marxist philosophy. He reports that agriculture is in a deplorable condition, and is so recognized by the Kremlin. He would not be surprised to see something in the nature of the American mechanized family farm replace the present state farms, if Kosygin's reforms prove successful in industry. This would be another long step toward a mixed economy.

The demand for motorcars, TV sets, and other durable goods for consumers was strong when I was last in Russia. Since then it has become a tidal wave. It is this demand from the rank and file which is partly responsible for the reforms in industry. Another reason is the rise of a new school of economists, led by Professor Lieberman of Kharkov. He is advocating—right out loud in *Pravda*—more and better goods for consumers, more attention to profits, to interest on capital, to eliminating incompetent workers, and to rewarding efficient managers.

Lieberman has put efficiency ahead of the class struggle, which under Stalin surely would have landed him in Siberia. Yet this trend is not too surprising, after all, when we remember that Russia now graduates more engineers and technologists than the United States, and that her achievements in both weaponry and space research are remarkable. A mind trained in the scientific method has some difficulty in reversing all its gears to think like a Marxist. You can't land a man on the moon with dialectical materialism.

I believe it obvious that as science advances, rigid Marxism must retreat. China has only a few top scientists today and Marxism is dominant, not to say violent. Give China another decade while she tries to catch up with Western technology, and her ideological convictions, like those of the Russians, may suffer considerable change.

The satellite nations in Europe have been moving toward a mixed economy even more rapidly than Russia. Rumania seems to be farthest along as I write, but Poland, East Germany, Czechoslovakia, and Bulgaria have all been breaking away from rigid central planning, and experimenting with market devices in both industry and agriculture. Yugoslavia, though not a satellite, is definitely on the same trend curve. Poland's chief economic planner proclaimed in 1965 that consumer demand and industrial profit "must henceforth guide Poland's economy." He went on cautiously to say, before a closed session of the Central Committee of the Communist Party in Warsaw: "Planning is the main advantage of the socialist system over capitalism. But we must introduce methods that will lead to an optimal harmony between central planning and industrial initiative at lower levels." "Optimal harmony"—a better term for the virtues of a mixed economy would be difficult to find.

Along with this trend has gone the collapse of monolithic political Communism. Russia and China are in a bitter power struggle as to which will lead the movement, and a world apart in their interpretation of Marxism-Leninism. "We must have peaceful coexistence or face incineration," says Moscow. "No truce with the capitalist-imperialists!" shouts Peking. Yugoslavia was the first to break away from the Kremlin, and now we find variations of Communist doctrine in Albania, North Vietnam, North Korea, Cuba, as well as in the satellites. Rather than a monolithic bloc, the semanticist would label them as separate belligerent nations, adhering to a series of ideologies—Communism$_1$, Communism$_2$, Communism$_3$, and so on to Communism$_n$—all claiming the true faith, and the true interpretation of the sacred writings. It reminds one of the break-up of monolithic Catholicism in the sixteenth century, with Tito, rather than Martin Luther, nailing the 91 articles to the cathedral door.

George Kennan has used the word "polycentrism" (many centers) to describe the current disarray of the Communist movement. Any attempt, he says, to establish either Moscow or Peking as the unchallenged center would involve prohibitive strains among the faithful; it would cause the whole Communist world "to break violently apart." Every Communist party today, he says, is afflicted by sharp internal differences, and is caught up in a great crisis of indecision over the correct attitude toward non-Communist nations. But this well-documented crisis seems to have little effect on the United States Congress: "They're Communists, aren't they?" If the word is there, the thing must be there too, and so a verbal monolith is buttressed against the facts of polycentrism.

John H. Kautsky, writing in *Current*,[2] carries the concept a step further. The failure to admit the depth of the split between Russia and China illustrates, he says, the familiar myth of the *single enemy*. People confronted with a complex situation, and unable to analyze the complexity, reduce it to plain black or white. Thus:

To Nazis, all opposition, no matter what the source, was a Jewish conspiracy.

To Stalin, all opposition was a capitalist conspiracy.

To Mao, all enemies, including the Soviet Union, are capitalist-imperialists.

To members of the John Birch Society, one might add, everything from the United Nations to the fluoridation of town

[2] July, 1965.

water is a Communist conspiracy. (When you hear the word "conspiracy" in a political argument, the chances are excellent that the speaker is in an ideological fog.)

The U.S.S.R., Kautsky believes, is being forced by technology into the economic patterns of open societies, and the cold war will gradually decline.

For all their theological differences, every one of the "Communist" countries, except possibly China, is on the road to a mixed economy. If China really desires to increase production and feed her people, she will have to march the same way. This is where every open society is marching—but by a different route. The closed societies are encouraging more local initiative and profit incentives; the open societies are going in for more fiscal and monetary planning, together with more controls over the physical environment.

"If the world's great religions, like Islam and Christianity, after a prolonged and bloody war for centuries, can flourish side by side in peace and amity, why should not Communist and non-Communist systems be permitted to co-exist peacefully?" U Thant raised this question in an eloquent passage, and technology is underwriting it. Why should we not expect this world-wide trend toward a more efficient way of producing goods? Both closed and open societies, under conditions of high energy, are in the grip of something more demanding than the nineteenth-century doctrines of David Ricardo or Karl Marx. They must both work with the imperatives of technology, its liabilities as well as its assets. They must both deal with the population explosion and the threat of nuclear war. If the trends in open and closed societies could be plotted, it is anybody's guess whether they would not someday meet, leaving East and West with many similar economic institutions. But there is not a shadow of a doubt about the direction, no doubt at all about the force which guides them. Economic interdependence, mass production, computerization, systems analysis, management psychology, all are implicit in an economy of abundance, whatever the local ideology.

When cheap nuclear energy is widely available, the trend to a mixed economy will be speeded up, and the division between capitalism and Communism further weakened. The prophecy of Keynes, that there will be no economic problem a century hence because production will then be so abundant, should be close to fulfillment.

9

AUTOMATION AND COMPUTERS

THE American telephone industry has calculated that if dialing and other automatic devices had not been developed in the Bell Laboratories, it would require the entire female population of the country, at the old switchboards, to handle the present volume of calls. A more dramatic case to illustrate the labor-saving potential of automation would be hard to find.

Peaceful energy from the atom and the advance of a mixed economy are technological trends which seem to promise well for the human condition. With automation, however, the net effect, certainly for the moment, is more clouded. Many Americans are losing their jobs to labor-saving devices, especially the computer—some estimates run as high as a million jobs a year—and the word "automation" has acquired an ugly connotation. A typical cartoon shows two observers halted beside a factory. Looking up they see workers catapulted through the air from every window. "Ah," the legend runs, "Jones and Company are automating!"

In West Germany, by way of contrast, labor-saving devices have been welcomed, in the face of a labor shortage so acute that workers were imported in wholesale lots. When the millionth foreign worker, a carpenter from Portugal, arrived in Cologne in 1964, he was met with a brass band, a laurel wreath, and the present of a motor scooter.

Automation, in one view, is an assault on human nature. Man is a working animal, it is alleged, and will degenerate rapidly if deprived of purposeful activity. I suspect Jacques Ellul would agree. In another view, man is a creative animal. Machines and computers can liberate his creative instincts by performing various dull, repetitive tasks which have handicapped him down the ages. Consider the galley slave, and the man on the assembly line.

A DEFINITION

So goes the argument. Well, let us see. First of all, what do we mean by "automation"? John Diebold is said to have coined the term in the 1950's for a mechanical operation which was automatic and self-regulating. He said:

Automation means something more than a mere extension of mechanization. . . . It implies a basic change toward the manner of performing work. All previous mechanizations depended on the reaction time of a human being—fingers, arms, height, the temperature a man could stand. . . . Now, through the principle called *feedback,* machines can be built which control their own operation, so that production does not have to take into account the limitations of a human worker.

This is a profound distinction. The machine has a built-in element that holds the machine strictly to its task. The man no longer needs to guide it; he can go out to lunch. In simplest terms, a feedback permits the machine to ask itself, "How am I doing?"—and then if necessary correct its own course. The standard illustration of a feedback is the thermostat governing the oil burner which heats a house. When the room grows too cold, the thermostat turns the burner on and, when the room is well heated, turns it off. This sequence continues all night while the household sleeps. Another classic example, suggested to me by an engineer who worked on it, Hans Asmussen, is the gyroscopic ship stabilizer, that detects the slightest roll and offsets it before a big roll can build up. Feedbacks can be activated by pressure, light, sound, and radiation, as well as by movement and temperature.

Thus "automation," in the sense of self-regulation, was around long before Diebold gave it a name. Even the vane on a primitive windmill, holding the face to the prevailing wind, is a feedback. It is interesting to note that social scientists, studying group dynamics, have adopted the term "feedback" for the process in which they halt the discussion and summarize its progress: "How are we doing?" The computer, of course, has carried self-regulation to unprecedented heights, as we shall see.

The term "automation," however, has long since escaped from the precise sense of self-regulation, and is now used for practically any mechanism which saves human labor. Henry Ford's first use of an assembly line is confidently called automation; so are a bulldozer, a printing press, a traveling crane. A wheelbarrow could be an example of automation by this more catholic definition; one man at the handles replaces two men with loads on their backs. As a student of semantics, I am loath to see a good term so adulterated—but there it is.

Earlier, Norbert Wiener, working on computers at MIT, had coined the term "cybernetics"—from the Greek word for steersman—for mechanisms and processes which steered themselves. In common usage, however, it cannot compete with "automation."

A CONTRAST

Ford's assembly line saved an enormous amount of labor, and brought the cost of a model T (which you could order in any color provided it was black) below $1,000. But men stood along the moving conveyor belt, and each bolted home one part—say, the left front fender. The creative urge was allowed no outlet; indeed the literati gave a special derogatory label to the men performing monotonous labor to the dictates of a machine: "robots," they were called.

About a dozen years after the robots went to work in Detroit, true automation as defined by Diebold was developed in the A. O. Smith plant in Milwaukee, which produced steel frames for automobiles. There were 26 stations along the moving line, where a piece of sheet steel was converted into a frame for, say, a Chevrolet. But on 25 of these stations not a man was to be seen. The work had been truly automated—in a kind of Charlie Chaplin inferno. Writing about it for *Fortune,* I said:

> We enter a door and are suddenly drowned in sound. We are in a vast room, perhaps 300 feet long and 200 wide, with walls of glass. Its floor is a mass of glittering steel, a thousand shapes which rush and stop, rise and fall, advance and retreat, dancing to some gigantic rhythm, yet to a counterpoint which sets up no vibration. . . . One hour and one-half from raw steel to freight car. Every eight seconds a completed frame, 420 an hour, 10,000 a day.

Two thousand workers were cut to 200 by true automation in this factory. The cost of building the automated plant with all its feedbacks was of course far greater than the cost of a plant designed for human robots. Today, when a series of computers controls an automated factory, the noise is less and the mechanisms more deft. When I visited A. O. Smith, with hands over my ears, electronic computers had not been invented.

HISTORICAL

Before tangling with the exponential advance of computers, let us consider briefly the historical sequence in labor-saving devices.

1. Hand tools, beginning with the caveman's fist ax, came

first many thousands of years ago.

2. Various mechanisms gradually were invented to replace some hand tools—water mills, windmills, primitive pumps, grinding machines. The sailing ship displaced galley slaves, at a great saving of labor.

3. Energy from coal, and presently oil, displaced wind, falling water, and animals, to power the procession of mechanisms which made up the first industrial revolution. The steam engine of James Watt, which went to work in 1776, was its symbol. But men, women, and children spent long, dreary hours tending the new machines, especially in the manufacture of textiles.

> The golf links lie so near the mill
> That almost every day
> The children standing at their work
> Can see the men at play

4. Mass production, beginning with the manufacture of rifles for the United States Army early in the nineteenth century, and culminating in assembly lines manned by human robots, multiplied the efficiency of mechanical energy.

5. True automation now removes the human worker altogether. Production is self-regulating, on the feedback principle. Specialists control and repair the process, but do not handle the product.

THE SECOND INDUSTRIAL REVOLUTION

True automation is often called the second industrial revolution because of its elimination of *mental* work. It attacks the white-collar bank clerk as well as the blue-collar machine tender. What is left for the man? A series of skilled operations are left for him, including:

The design of the mechanism.
The programming of computers including logic design; getting them ready to go to work. One estimate indicates that by 1975 there will

be more programmers in the United States than doctors.
The maintenance and repair of the mechanism.
The interpretation and communication of results.

Observe that the robot has no place in this sequence; the assembly line has disappeared. Tasks are highly specialized and very well paid; many require a college degree, if not a Ph.D.

These processes are a long way from a fist ax, a long way from the "dark, satanic mills" of Lancashire and Lawrence. But the output of goods and services will require a constantly declining number of man-hours as the computer takes over. Some observers, speaking of the present, call it not the *nuclear age* but the *computer age*. It may be not without significance that the first models for electronic computers arrived in the same year as the destruction of Hiroshima. The computers were designed to speed statistical calculations required for the war.

There are two kinds of computers, analogue and digital. The first responds to physical events, temperature, pressure, motion, and is thus *analogous* to these events. The speedometer on your car is a simple analogue, transforming the revolution of the car's wheels into miles per hour. The odometer on an airplane, however, responding to the distance already traversed, belongs to the digital family. Most of the computers now being manufactured are digitals, and we will confine the discussion to them.

DIGITAL COMPUTERS

Back in 1953, in connection with a study I was making in communication theory, I interviewed No. 701 of International Business Machines, the latest on the market at the time. It was a digital computer, filling a large room with many cabinets flashing colored lights. It was said to be 25 times faster than the early Mark I, at Harvard. I discovered, somewhat to my chagrin, that No. 701 could multiply four digits by four digits 100,000 times faster than I could! That is saying it was 10^5 faster. Now, in 1967, the speed is 10^8, or 100 million times faster than a normal man can multiply. The new models, indeed, are said to be 10 times smaller (because of the substitution of transistors for bulky vacuum tubes), 1,000 times cheaper and 100 times faster than the computers of a decade ago. A machine the size of a kitchen refrigerator can do the work of one which filled a whole floor 15 years ago. It is confidently expected that a decade hence a similar exponential advance will be registered in computer technology.

The digital computer reduces the ten digits, 0 to 9, of our standard decimal system to two symbols, 0 and 1, corresponding to the *"off"* and *"on"* of an electric current. By means of complicated wired connections (the business of the programmer and the logic designer) many variable quantities— distance, direction, speed, age, years in school, individual scores, even ledger accounts—expressed in terms of these two symbols, can be stored, correlated, and manipulated. The current can then flick around the programmed circuits at a speed not far from that of light. It is this monstrous speed which permits the fantastic rate of adding, multiplying, and dividing, 100 million times faster than a normal human brain.

Digital computers can also handle letters of the alphabet, or other symbols, by encoding them in what the engineers call binary "bits." A "bit" is the smallest event in communication theory, an historic concept worked out by Claude Shannon in the Bell Laboratories.[1] In a 7-bit code, 0100000 stands for the letter A. Someday soon, it is predicted, computers will be able to handle oral bits. Then we can talk to a computer and it will talk back.

Any number can be expressed in terms of just two symbols,

[1] Claude Shannon and Warren Weaver, *The Mathematical Theory of Communication,* University of Illinois Press, 1949.

by changing their order and repeating them. If the symbols are 0 and 1, then let 1 stand for one, 10 stand for two, 11 stand for three, 100 stand for four (which is two squared), and, continuing along, 1101 stand for thirteen—a perfectly regular, logical system in which any of our more familiar decimal system numbers can be expressed. Its trouble for human beings is the very large number of 0's and 1's needed as we go up the scale. This is called the *binary*, or base-two, system. If you are interested, you can construct a base-three system, or a base-four system, or a five- or an eight-baser.

After performing its calculations in binary, a well-mannered computer can translate the results back to our standard base-ten system with its decimal numbers, and neatly type the answer. A computer has five major parts:

1. *Input* section, where we find punch card readers, tape readers, and other processors to translate various signals.

2. *Calculation*, the "main frame" unit, where the mathematics goes over the circuits at blinding speed.

3. *Storage or memory* units, where the input can be held in reserve for almost instant reference. This section is increasingly important for "data processing"—as we shall presently see in the case of a bank.

4. *Control unit*, where a man may stand at the console, equipped with dials like those on the dashboard of a motorcar, starting, stopping, or checking the whole process.

5. *Output*, where the answer appears, typewritten, or otherwise reproduced for interpretation. Someday it may be spoken.

The latest models all have feedbacks, with which the computer can assess its own performance and correct its mistakes. "Centers" are now being established where a big computer can handle a number of clients, such as a hospital, a university, a factory, or a string of branch banks. These centers are thus becoming a kind of public utility, like the telephone service.

The trend in modern industry for half a century has been to

substitute the human nervous system for human muscle. Computers take the process a long step further; they replace the human nervous system by electronic impulses. They can solve in minutes an equation which would take years of paper work if done by a man. In a recent mission in space, for instance, a computer in the capsule "performed as many calculations governing the mission as one man could make by hand in four years." The rendezvous of two spacecraft in orbit is impossible without computer control, and it is impossible for a man to get to the moon without such rendezvous.

Before we credit digital computers with unlimited intelligence, however, let us listen to a man who is on intimate terms with them, John Morris of the Computer Institute at Michigan State:

Of course, the computer is *not* a human being, and a sequence of pulses through its wires is *not* a human thought. A computer is incredibly fast, but, in some ways, it is distressingly stupid. It lacks the common sense we like to attribute to human beings. Once off on a wrong scent, it can never, of its own volition, come back to the right one. . . . A big computer can make a million "decisions" a second, but these resemble human decisions only to the extent that an electric light switch resembles Hamlet meditating "To be or not to be. . . ."

At the same time a computer's operations do bear some resemblance to human thinking, because this is precisely what they were intended to do. A computer is designed to operate very rapidly on problems that have been developed by people in order to provide results that will be useful to people. Its "thinking" is Aristotelian, in the sense that each problem is eventually resolved into a sequence of two-valued "decisions" [i.e., either *on* or *off*].

COMPUTER IN A BANK

Up to about 1900, clerks on high stools, with green eye-shades, kept the accounts of bank depositors in big ledgers with pen and ink. A few years later bookkeeping machines were introduced, and the clerk discarded pen and ink to punch various keys arranged like a typewriter. This operation displaced about half the clerks, but it was not true automation. Today a computer with an operator at the console not only runs the depositors' ledgers, but makes out their monthly statements. This is true automation, where *all the bookkeepers have disappeared*. One large New York bank, after installing the "Magnetic Ink Character Recognition System" for recording checks by computer, eliminated the 144 bookkeepers who had been operating machines.

The hieroglyphics which now appear on your checks belong to the "magnetic character" system, and permit the computer to identify each depositor. Here is what happens in my bank, where a computer keeps track of my account.

I step to the teller's wicket in one of the branches and cash a personal check for $50. Later in the day it is photographed and the amount imprinted, and it is sent with other checks by messenger to a Data Processing Center in a town 20 miles away. Here it is stacked with other checks at the right-hand side of a "reader-sorter," a big steel cabinet. A button is pushed and the checks whirl through this cabinet, to drop down in slots below. Then the data are transferred to the "memory" section by means of magnetic tape recorders, which file each check under the depositor's personal number. A battery of these recorders stand in the center of a 60-foot room, looking like tall gasoline pumps with clock faces, their hands usually in motion. Other strange constructs hum and click and flash and turn, but not so noisily as to prevent me from asking questions. I find this a great improvement over the frame-mill inferno of the A. O. Smith Company. Half a dozen young men stroll casually around, ready to make adjustments if a machine signals for attention.

One of the machines, looking something like a kitchen dishwasher, is pointed out by my guide as the "memory" section.

It has engulfed the account of every depositor in every branch. My $50 check has been duly debited to my account, and all my deposit slips credited. At the same time the bank's general ledger is debited and credited daily with the sum total of all depositors' accounts. The computer thus runs both detail and general accounts.

At the end of a given monthly period, the output section, going like a November gale, will type a record of my account, and everybody else's account, which will then be mailed with all canceled checks. I receive my statement on the 18th, no longer on the first of the month. To send everybody his statement on the first, I am told, would give the computer a nervous breakdown.

They also tell me at the Center that they are going to put the computer to work recording mortgages. This will require a long period of programming by high-powered specialists. I also learn that the two best programmers in my bank come from Yale; one majored in physics, the other in English literature.

"What have they in common?" I inquire.

"Logic," my guide replies.

HOSPITALS

Here is a man being admitted to a local hospital. He shows his Blue Cross card to the admissions clerk. She types an inquiry on an electronic teleprinter, which cuts it into punched tape. The tape then transmits it by wire to the Blue Cross computer in another city. The computer unprotestingly interrupts whatever it is doing and searches its memory unit for the patient's record. In *just two seconds,* the coded record is transmitted back to the hospital, allowing the clerk to complete her business with the new patient in less than three minutes. It used to take from two to four days when the inquiry was sent by mail. If the patient came in only for his annual checkup, he might have been discharged, under the old system, before his Blue Cross record was cleared. Observe that there is no multiplying and dividing in this case of data processing.

RESCUE AT SEA

Day by day, almost hour by hour, new uses are being found for computers. On a stormy night in mid-Atlantic a cabin boy fell in the engine room of a freighter and was badly hurt. There was no doctor aboard. A distress call went out over the radio, to be picked up by the U.S. Coast Guard in New York. The officer on duty glanced at his chart; the ship was 2,000 miles away and no Coast Guard vessel could possibly reach her in time. But somewhere in that area should be a ship which *did* have a doctor. What ship, where? The officer called the AMVER (Atlantic Merchant Vessel Report), giving the freighter's position. A punched card was fed into AMVER's computer, whose "memory" held a record of 800 ships then crossing the Atlantic. The computer calculated their positions, then typed a list of all ships with doctors in the vicinity of the freighter. The Coast Guard officer radioed the ship, and a rendezvous was arranged with a nearby French liner. Less than two hours after the accident, the two ships met, at a position calculated by the computer. The boy was transferred to the liner, where a skilled surgeon saved his life. . . . Yet many people call automation inhuman.

PRINTING

Lord Thomson of Fleet Street in 1965 touched a button which started the presses of one of his local papers—the first newspaper ever printed to combine computer control, photographic typesetting, and offset color printing. It will not be the last. Said Lord Thomson: "I can envisage one big computer capable of setting type for the whole of England." When asked about the compositors and others displaced when the *Evening*

Post automated, all he could do was to hope for the best. Great newspapers in America are now shaken, strike-bound, and even put out of business by this question.

CRIME

The task of anticipating crime has been taken over by a computer in Chicago. Spot information on suspicious or criminal activity is fed into it, and within minutes it ejects an analysis of areas in the city, and types of crime, which require immediate attention. The police force is alerted for action. This job used to be left to precinct officers, who took four days to submit a report.

Computers are making life difficult for income tax evaders too, by remembering everything done or left undone on previous returns. Other computers are beginning to make life more cheerful for poor families in Appalachia, where the number of miners has fallen from 419,000 in 1947 to 180,000 in the mid-sixties—the result of mechanization. By codifying the data, agents can make relief payments much more rapidly and equitably.

SEARCHING THE LAW

Computers are making life easier for lawyers and judges. As the cases pile up over the years, the task of finding precedents becomes ever more arduous. Sometimes it becomes too arduous for a judge to review all past decisions. Belgium is now turning this boring and time-consuming task over to a computer—mindful of what Voltaire once said about the drawbacks of the law: "the profusion of useless things one has to keep in one's head."

With a computer service called "credoc," a lawyer called on, say, to handle the sale of a piece of property by the legal guardian of a child, can put in a call to credoc and in a few minutes receive all the references—statutes, previous judge-ments, learned studies—which otherwise would have taken him days of tiresome research.

A similar service is proposed for scientific papers. Who has worked on this question before? A computer can tell quickly and precisely.

A MASSIVE TREND

Computers will soon be at work in the field of preventive medicine, undertaking diagnosis, and saving the time of doctors, technicians, and nurses. They can aid the learning process in school, by permitting children to proceed at their own pace rather than by class standardization. Middle management, however, seems to be in for a rough future as computers take over the logic of decision-making. A computer is not bothered by personal feelings or opinions, and can dispense a tough brand of practical logic on the either/or basis. Program the variables in the problem, turn on the power, and out comes the most logical decision.

Despite some hazards and some appalling lapses now and then,[2] the deep human motive of "least work," to say nothing of least cost, is so compelling that the trend to automation cannot be stopped. Said Adlai Stevenson:

> The image of the automation engineer may not excite the imagination as does the image of the astronaut, but the fate of mankind in the foreseeable future will depend more on what we do manipulating machines here on earth than on how we do hurtling them through the heavens.

FORMULA FOR AUTOMATING

If automation cannot be stopped in the long run, the labor unions which are trying to stop it now are obviously wasting

[2] The Manufacturers Hanover Trust Company in New York was paralyzed in November, 1965, when the computer broke down which controlled both depositors' accounts and personal loans. It took four experts all night to fix it. This could not happen with human bookkeepers.

their energy and their bank accounts, to say nothing of infuriating the public. Featherbedding has no future. These high generalizations, however, are not very meaningful to the man about to lose his job; is there no way to soften the blow?

There is a way: a rough formula is emerging. An organization, before it converts, must be prepared *neither to fire nor hire* (except for specialists). All regular workers are kept on the payroll, whether working or not, but no new ones are hired. Strenuous efforts are made to retrain and relocate a displaced worker, but if a niche cannot be found, he is kept on at the old salary. As workers retire or leave voluntarily, total payroll will come down. As automation increases production, and hopefully sales, some pensioners go back to work. As business continues to increase, new workers will be hired. This is drastic medicine, but it makes sense. The Kaiser Steel Company, among others, has experimented with the formula successfully.

Some experts predict that a generation hence automation will be opening up more jobs than it is destroying, by virtue of industries and services now unknown. And it may be, as suggested earlier, that the reconstruction of our ailing cities, together with programs to reduce air and water pollution, will create millions of new jobs, both manual and mental. Until such a happy future comes into better focus, however, there is going to be great trouble, which only the most careful forward planning by unions, managements, and government can avert. Even if a new job opens up, a man who has given years of his life to a specialty faces a serious human problem. Can he be retrained, and by whom? Must he shift his home and family to another part of the country?

Sighting along the trend curve raises other difficult questions. Even if many new jobs are created in the next decade or two, will they continue to rise? Will not the expansion of automation overrun them in the end? Even if a living wage is paid to every citizen whether he works or not, what will be the psychological effects of prolonged leisure? *Is man a working animal?* This question is so fundamental that we will give the next chapter to its discussion.

Again, how will automation affect education? Most American boys hitherto have gone to college with the goal of earning a living. Well below the graduation oratory of the "all-around man" and the "well-stocked mind," an income-producing job has been the real goal. What happens when the goal is undermined by automation? It is said that many undergraduates in American colleges today are wavering about going into private business. For the long run, a curriculum geared to the liberal arts, and a clearer understanding of oneself and one's world, doubtless provides a loftier goal than making money. For the short run, however, it could generate an educational revolution. In Chapter 15 we will go deeper into this.

Automation is well under way in the United States and in Canada, with some unfortunate results as company after company converts. It is gathering momentum in Western Europe, Britain, and Japan, and sooner or later is bound to create unemployment there. Russia and her allies may be next in line. Automation is a function of the mixed economy toward which all high-energy societies are moving, as we have seen. It will be aided and abetted, too, by cheaper power from the atom.

The Research Institute of America in New York has summarized the massive shift in ominous words:

The whole definition of "work" itself is beginning to change. As workers become less producers and more watchers of machines, there will be new problems of morale, boredom, frustration . . . *time* is overtaking money as a basic form of wealth. That is the really crucial fact about the automation revolution that no one has faced squarely yet—that payment in *leisure* may become as important as payment in goods.

Students of automation have also predicted that within a decade or so a computer will be the world's chess champion, the discoverer of an important new theorem in mathematics, the composer of some acceptable music. Perhaps—such prospects make a good cover story for any magazine. What is really important, however, is not a few stunts hitherto in the realm of science fiction, but the transcendent effect on human work and human leisure.

Finally, let me emphasize once more that a computer is just a piece of hardware until a programmer—a man—first tells it what to do, in a special computer language, and then plugs in the power. It can then, if well designed, do what it is told much faster and more accurately than any man. It can hold to a simple logical line more obstinately than any man. But nothing comes out of it which a man has not first put in.

Richard Bellman, writing in *Science* about "dynamic programming" where computers are mandatory, makes this penetrating observation: In dealing with another person or with a human group "we can enjoy the luxury of being irrational, illogical, inconsistent and incomplete, but in operating a computer we must meet the rigorous requirements for detailed instructions and absolute precision." A computer, you see, though it cannot think, can tighten up a man's thinking to a remarkable degree.

☆

10

IS MAN A WORKING ANIMAL?

COMPUTERS and automatic mechanisms have already taken over a great deal of routine work, such as bank bookkeeping, and they are expected to take over a great deal more. Not only large plants and offices will be computerized, but also small organizations, as the hardware becomes less costly.

What then will happen to *people?* Uncounted thousands have already lost their employment to automation; other thousands are postponing the event through crippling strikes on the railroads, the docks, and in newspapers and printing plants. Gerard Piel estimates that if hours had *not* come down below 60 a week, there would now be 27 million unemployed in the United States.

If people have no jobs, how can they buy the products made by the workers who remain? If, on the other hand, it is possible to subsidize the jobless as consumers, what happens to their nervous systems, self-confidence, and character? Most of us would rather be occupied than not, as I shall try to demonstrate, but in what form? There are three main possibilities:

1. By "having fun," by sight-seeing, tropical cruises, and consuming *furioso*. The "jet set" provides a model.

2. By finding new varieties of economic work on a regular payroll, such as rebuilding Megalopolis.

3. By expanding noneconomic occupations, such as serious

hobbies, amateur arts, community activities on unpaid town boards, and the like.

We will examine these alternatives later in the chapter. Meanwhile let us see what happens to some people who have money but no work, and to others who have work which they dislike extremely. There are a number of reliable studies which throw light on man and his occupations.

SOME CASES

A few years ago I acted as consultant in a survey of male employees, both blue-collar and white-, who had been retired at age 65 from one of America's largest corporations. From chairman of the board down to janitor they had to quit. How were they getting on? They had few financial problems, thanks to the company's generous pension system. They were primarily in the money-but-no-work class.

Some got into the family car on retirement and headed for Florida or California, glad to be rid of the daily grind—or so they thought. In six months most of them were back in New York. Those with well-developed hobbies, or part-time business interests, were usually all right; those with nothing to involve them deeply were often in trouble. Some had mental breakdowns; one committed suicide. Another—perhaps the saddest case on the record—set his alarm clock at the habitual hour and went every morning to the old shop to watch the other men do what he once did.

As a result of the survey, the company set up a panel of psychiatric counsellors to help employees who were approaching retirement to find activities which could hold their interest when the regular job expired. Leisure with an adequate income, but without involvement, had been found a disintegrating experience for all too many, despite their age. If this happened to older men at 65, what would happen to more vigorous men at 35 or 40? In the light of this study, man seemed indeed to be a working animal.

The Secretary of Health, Education and Welfare, John W. Gardner, has called for "mid-career clinics" to prepare middle-aged workers for their retirement—"one of life's toughest adjustments." He points out that the typical man retiring at 65 can expect 25,000 hours of extra time for the rest of his life, "a vast amount either for constructive use or aimless boredom." Secretary Gardner wants management, unions, and universities to cooperate in setting up clinics to keep life meaningful after retirement.

John Wilkinson, of the Center for the Study of Democratic Institutions at Santa Barbara, has reported on what took place when automation invaded the great oil refineries in the Middle East. Tribesmen who had jobs in the refineries lost their work but not their comforts and amenities; income continued. King Ibn Saud complained to the oil companies that the men were sitting around doing nothing and growing dangerously restless. They had schools, hospitals, and air-conditioned homes; but their idleness, said Saud, was making for a "potentially violent revolutionary situation." He urged the engineers to put the men back on the floor and find something for them to do. The company, however, feared that men on the floor might interfere with the automated process, and then the refinery itself might have a nervous breakdown.

In the 1960's workers in American steel mills won a 13-week paid vacation for veteran employees, in their union contract. This was hailed as a great victory, but did not prove very successful. While some of the workers pursued interesting hobbies which they had developed earlier, "many others complained that they just didn't know what to do with all that time."

The Council on Aging corroborates this complaint. It finds three difficulties with uninterrupted leisure, especially for the less educated:

1. Most American workers are simply not prepared to shift

from an established routine to "uncharted hours of retirement." Many low-income workers regard the learning of hobbies with contempt. They have not developed outside interests
during their working life, and boredom, suffered in the past
only on weekends, comes to spread a blight over the months
and years of retirement.

2. In a work-oriented culture, the Council continues, the
loss of identity with the job can devastate a worker's self-
respect. He comes to think of retirement as akin to the shame
of unemployment.

3. Retirement can also disrupt a comfortable lifetime relationship between man and wife. When the husband sits around
the house all day with little to do, deeply grooved habits are
disturbed and family quarrels develop.

The Council on Aging pointedly asks if a rule for arbitrary
retirement at 60 or 65 is worth these three risks.

Arthur L. Schlesinger, Jr., the historian, is even more
emphatic. "The most dangerous threat hanging over American society," he says, "is the threat of leisure . . . and those
who have the least preparation for it will have the most of it."
One may question his priority—there are other serious threats
in American society—but he is quite right in identifying the
group which will suffer most if and when automation creates a
serious vacuum in the job market. It will be those citizens who
have developed only limited interests outside the job, or no
interests at all.

Novelists and storytellers since time out of mind have a
stock character in the profligate son, who lives on the family
inheritance and has nothing to do but gamble, drink, and
seduce the innocent. The plain moral, that money without
work is corrupting, may derive more from the Puritan ethic
than from sound sociology, but great novelists, such as
Tolstoy, have used it. Most of us can recall such cases in our
personal acquaintance.

Kipling in *Barrack Room Ballads* draws a sharp picture of soldiers in peacetime, bored to death and getting into all kinds of trouble. "Drill, ye Terriers, drill!" They long for a war to give them some purpose in life. Even in wartime the interminable waiting around has been found disintegrating.

OPINION SURVEY

Dr. Robert L. Kahn of the University of Michigan asked a nationwide sample of American workers "whether or not they would continue to work even if, by some chance, they had enough money to satisfy all their needs." No less than 80 percent replied they would go right on working. Among the reasons: they wanted to keep occupied, to keep interested, to avoid being bored. "This finding," said Dr. Kahn, "is pretty general for most occupations and ages of the respondents, and argues a nearly universal need for work."

When the same respondents, however, were asked if they *liked* their present jobs, two-thirds of them said they did not. They wanted to go on working, yes, but at something else—preferably a little business of their own. "While work certainly seems necessary for a balanced emotional life," Dr. Kahn concludes, "many people are doing kinds of work which they don't want to do." In another opinion survey, in a large modern well-appointed plant, one apathetic worker told the interviewer: "The only satisfaction around here, Doc, is the old buck."

A study of 1,800 men on an automobile assembly line in Connecticut found only one man in 10 liking, or at least not disliking, his job.[1] The belt was heartily resented by 90 percent. The resentment arose primarily because the whole process was preplanned, giving the worker no responsibility for the pace of his labor or its content. Nor was there a chance for

[1] Charles Walker and Robert H. Guest, *The Man on the Assembly Line,* Harvard University Press, 1952.

the age-old motivation of teamwork. The man worked alone with almost no contact with his fellows. "We suggest," the report noted, "that the sense of becoming depersonalized is, for those who feel it, a psychologically more disturbing result than the boredom." When the line occasionally broke down, a great spontaneous "Hurrah!" filled the plant. Many said that they were bored to the limit of endurance. "The job is so sickening, day in and day out plugging in ignition wires. I get through one motor, turn around, and there's another one staring me in the face."

Norbert Wiener, the father of cybernetics, feels for the man on the assembly line. It is a humiliation, he says, for a human being to be chained to a galley and used as a source of power; but it is equally humiliating to ask a worker in a factory to repeat over and over again an action which requires only one-millionth of the capacity of his brain for its fulfillment.[2]

WHAT DO THEY WANT TO DO?

That men want to work seems pretty clear in the light of the above evidence, but not always at what they are doing. There is work and work. We remember Art Young's famous cartoon of a laborer stumbling into his kitchen after a hot summer day. He says to his wife, "By gorry, I'm tired." She replies, "There you go! You're tired! Here I be a-standin' over a hot stove all day, and you're workin' in a nice cool sewer!"

Asked to define "work," about half the respondents in the Kahn survey just cited said that work was something one has to do, or something one doesn't like to do. We have here, of course, prime evidence of the strong Puritan ethic in our culture. Painful things are good for one, pleasurable things are bad, and Satan always finds employment for idle hands.

The chief definition of "work" in American history has

---

[2] *The Human Use of Human Beings: Cybernetics and Society,* Houghton Mifflin, 1950.

been a condition where one is earning a living in field, factory, office, or bringing up a family. It is dubious, under this canon, whether I am working or not as I write these words; artists and writers have been suspect as useful producers since pioneer days. American males over age 50 have been reared on this ethic. Even if we were rich enough to be spared earning a living, we were careful to present substitute credentials. I used to visit in a wealthy community where very few males had to work beyond galloping after foxes. To a man, however, they were at the station every workday morning to take the 8:15 for Boston. What they did in Boston would make an interesting study for a sociologist. After the ceremonial appearance at "the office" most of them came home early.

A farmer works in the fields all day and then returns to his house, turns on the light, and reads *True Stories*. The editor of *True Stories* works to a frantic deadline all day, then drives home for an hour's pleasant exercise in his flower garden. One man's work can be another man's leisure.

THERE IS WORK AND WORK

The Census lists hundreds of occupations on a spectrum between the exciting and pleasurable, on one hand, and the deadly dull, if not hateful, on the other. . . . "I turn around and there is another motor staring me in the face." Most human beings prefer some variety in their activities; minds and bodies have been shaped by evolution more for change than repetitive monotony. The factory system has taken a biological species, evolved in a free outdoor life, and forced it into a rigid environment controlled by clocks, bells, and whistles. No tribe from the North Cape to Patagonia ever tolerated anything like this. The machine age has built a cage of concrete and steel and put man in it, like an animal in a zoo. Some animals survive in zoos. Some die.

The real distinction, I believe, is between an activity which involves one's whole personality and a vacuum. If automation is to condemn more and more of us to existing in a vacuum, Dr. Schlesinger's prediction may well be justified. Dr. Joshua Lederberg, Nobel Prize winner in medicine, goes a step further. He says that the lack of useful occupation for many older women today "is a preview of the leisure society where work may become the prerogative of a chosen elite." Only the top brass will be lucky enough to have something useful to do! The boredom resulting from nonwork, he fears, may develop into a pernicious nervous disorder. "Perhaps the scientist, who works for the joy of it, will be the most nearly pre-adapted for that topsy-turvy world."[3]

We are not in that topsy-turvy world yet, but high-energy societies are making considerable progress in that direction. There is, of course, no question about the decline in the hours of payroll work, which have fallen from 84 hours a week— seven 12-hour days—at the beginning of the industrial revolution, to around 40. Clerical work is down from 48 to 35 hours, while American labor unions are demanding a 30-hour standard work week. Meanwhile Dr. Richard Bellman of the Rand Corporation makes the startling prediction that by the end of the century 2 percent of the United States labor force will be able to produce everything the country can consume. The Technocrats in their most romantic prophecies never equaled that figure.

Professor William Gombey delves a little deeper, and makes the sound point that we live in a whirling-dervish economy, keyed to compulsive consumption. Planned obsolescence and annual models, he says, tends to mask the problem for a time, but how long before unemployment due to automation becomes chronic and accelerating? It cannot be masked indefinitely.

Now let us return to the three possible occupations for those displaced by automation listed at the beginning of the chapter: fun, new fields for paid work, unpaid work.

[3] *Bulletin of the Atomic Scientists,* October, 1966.

HAVING FUN

Some observers predict that the growth of leisure will result in a flowering of art, culture, and philosophy. Others, including your author, are more dubious—at least without a lot of training for the candidates. How do many of us spend our leisure now? Russell Baker takes a look at "having fun" in Florida. The tourist season is in full swing, he says, and the motels are crowded. There are various places to which one can drive from the motels. Some fun-seekers drive into the swamps to see the alligators. The alligators have a stabilizing influence. They have been around for a long time, and help to offset the feeling that the whole state was built last week. Or one can drive to the beach and watch planes drag streamers above the breaking waves advertising cocktail lounges. He can also watch the surf toss the garbage back on the beach. Baker goes on:

Florida tourism is built on the theory that what we want to do with our leisure time is to invest it entirely in relishing the present moment. Its goal is total fun in total comfort . . . but they wind up by being total bores, and in the process pleasure is lost.[4]

It is not inconceivable that the total-fun contingent might have more fun running a straight furrow, or even an old-fashioned spinning wheel. If man is a working animal, total fun may turn out to be a total bore. It is ironic to note that while fun-makers watch the melon rinds and the pop bottles being tossed back on the beach, a few miles away, at Cape Kennedy, mankind is making its most concentrated and adventurous advance, preparing to land on the moon.

NEW FIELDS OF WORK

There seem to be two chief prospects for new fields of activity to keep us from the vacuum of total comfort and total fun.

[4] *New York Times*, August 9, 1964.

The first is the very considerable amount of work needed to make living space livable again—especially the reconstruction of Megalopolis and the control of pollutants.

Consider the task of transforming New York City into a livable environment. Consider building the 350 "new towns" Victor Gruen calls for. Consider all the proposals for high-speed mass transportation which are gathering on the agenda, with San Francisco and Tokyo leading the way. Consider the work involved in exchanging gasoline motors for vehicles powered by electric batteries or fuel cells.

NONECONOMIC WORK

This field is wide, but not any too well explored. It includes any activity which can seriously involve a human being and which is not primarily concerned with earning a living.

Art forms are expanding in the United States at an exponential rate—painting, music, the dance, the theater. Much of the product is pretty bad, some of it is done for publicity, but as Gifford Phillips has pointed out, there is no question about its dynamism, and the extent of involvement by budding young artists. In our small rural town in Connecticut we have painters and sculptors exhibiting in the local bank, the barbershop, and the dry cleaners. We have string quartets, the Choral Society, the Redding Players, and rehearsals for the symphony concert series given in the next town. Nobody, unless it be the supply trade, is making real money out of this activity. There is a direct correlation between the growth of these local arts and the growth of leisure time.

Is it possible for a whole community to become involved? I have visited villages in Mexico where nearly every family was producing fine craftsmanship—pottery, glass, silverwork, serapes, furniture. If this means anything—will anthropologists please check me?—it means that every normal human being is a potential craftsman, if not an artist. Ishi from the Stone Age was a master craftsman. The tendency must be in the pool of genes, ready for encouragement by the culture.

Again, take hobbies. Sports are expanding rapidly with leisure, and in many of them the player must participate, and not just sit before a TV screen watching someone else perform. The list is long and includes skiing, bowling, snorkling, surf-boarding, bird-watching, rock-climbing. Any one of these can be fun, and some present the bright face of danger. Collecting can also involve one—ship models, Sandwich glass, Mexican *santos*, stamps, coins, lusterwork.

Coming back to useful work, there is the vast field, discussed in an earlier chapter, of helping the Hungry World to its feet, of which the Peace Corps is a pioneer example. This work may pay a living wage, but is certainly not a profit-making enterprise. Its power will come from a combination of idealism and intelligence, especially in young men and women. Indeed, the idea may extend to a kind of universal Job Corps, where every youngster gives a disciplined year or more to going down into that nice cool sewer and doing some of the dirty work of the world, work which no machine can be designed to do. On this agenda, too, would be much hospital work, care of the aged, supervision of young children, first aid in emergencies, and a wide variety of conservation work, like the CCC camps of the 1930's. It was William James, in his historic essay, "The Moral Equivalent of War," who inaugurated the idea. Already a Job Corps is being experimented with in America for unemployed youngsters.

Education in America is still directed primarily to getting a job. "The more specifically education is directed to jobs," says Gerard Piel, "the more ineffective it is bound to be." The cure, he says, is deliberate training for "no-jobs," for the useful employment of leisure, training to make people more human. It will not be impossible, he thinks, to engineer the transition from a "working society" to a "learning society." A prime function of education should be to supply the intellectual tools and disciplines for an understanding of the problems which the world now faces. We have been brought up, Piel says, in the Horatio Alger ethic of working hard for a living, and it is as far out of date as *The Arabian Nights*.

IN CONCLUSION

I think that we are safe in concluding that automation and the computer will go on making it possible to produce more stuff with less human work. Unless the new occupations and activities just described follow a similar upward trend, we are in for chronic unemployment on an ever grander scale— "structural unemployment" is the technical term used by the economists.

We are reasonably safe in concluding that man is a working animal, in the sense of requiring some activity to interest and involve him, if not in the sense of the Puritan ethic. Without such involvement he is at a loss—if not, indeed, a mental case. What he does, however, hardly needs to follow the ethic of income-producing labor on farm or industrial payroll. A normal life can be seriously distorted by repetitive, monotonous labor.

We are reasonably safe in concluding that there will be enough new fields of work of the payroll variety to keep unemployment in bounds for years to come, especially the reconstruction of Megalopolis. Beyond that is the possibility of Peace Corps work, involvement in the arts and crafts, amateur science, and hobbies which can be more rewarding than watching the alligators in the swamps of Florida. These activities will take some special training, however. Indeed, as automation gains, it promises to shake traditional education to its foundation.

Also, as automation gains, one can readily understand the very human reason for featherbedding in certain traditional occupations. There is no solution, however, in "making work" that makes no sense; no solution in riding a locomotive cab when there is no coal to be shoveled; no solution in resetting type by hand for advertisements already printed by offset. Such "work" may be even more destructive to the personality than doing nothing at all. Dostoevsky made this point when he said: "If it were desired to crush a man completely, to punish him so severely that even the most hardened murderer would quail, it would only be needed to make his work pointless and absurd."

It will not solve the problem of work to subsidize every family which does not earn enough to meet the health and decency standards—now about $3,000 a year in the United States. Such subsidy, under the label of "negative income tax," is being widely debated, and even blessed by such a conservative economist as Dr. Milton Friedman. It is certainly more than justified for the children of the poor, but it can demoralize their parents—if the parents continue idle and uninvolved. Along with the negative income tax should go carefully planned opportunities for useful work in reducing public squalor.

When all is said and done, however, it is less serious to face the challenge of abundance than to face the prospect of a stripped planet, and a downward spiral into scarcity.

☆

11

THE ARMS RACE

OUR PLANET can be stripped by too many people exhausting its resources, or it can be stripped very suddenly by thermonuclear war. It is impossible to consider the trend to war in the nuclear age without also considering the trend to peace. The late Robert Oppenheimer called the dual movement "a great peril and a great hope"; Winston Churchill put it even more eloquently: "By a process of sublime irony the world will reach a stage where safety will be the sturdy child of terror, and survival the twin brother of annihilation."

In this chapter we will confront the face of terror, which as Churchill says must impel men of goodwill and imagination to understand and resist it. In a further chapter some constructive aspects, especially the United Nations, will be explored.

NOT ONLY NUCLEAR WEAPONS

The terror, we must never forget, comes not merely from thermonuclear bombs. Even if such weapons were completely disallowed, the several nations could not go back to tanks, fighter planes, TNT, and other conventional weapons. Nuclear bombs and their delivery systems happen for the moment to be at the crest of the wave, attracting practically all the publicity, but other sophisticated weapons are immediately behind them—the psychochemicals, the biologicals, the lasers.

Military weaponry, growing at an exponential rate since the first use of gunpowder, was sooner or later bound to run off the map—bound to develop an offense against which there was no defense. If it had not been the atomic bomb, it might have been new techniques in poison gas dispersion, the spreading of plagues, death rays, or even mass hypnosis—all classified subjects in the Pentagon, but reported to be in active development.

The nerve gases, such as Tabun, Sarin, and Soman, go far beyond putting an enemy comfortably to sleep. Some are lethal, and others can cause permanent nerve damage. One variety of the psychochemicals can make a cat afraid of a mouse. The new lasers, which concentrate light waves, approximate the "death ray" dreamed up years ago by H. G. Wells. His invaders from Mars had mastered solid-state physics.

Technology has at last brought us to a point where modern strategic weapons cannot be used without recoiling on the user. Rather than victory or defeat, such weaponry now presents us with mutual suicide. This impasse was inevitable on the ascending curve of military technology, which is still being vigorously developed by all the great powers. Some techniques, such as the biologicals, can be manufactured cheaply, and may soon be available to the lesser powers—Guatemala, say, or Guinea. If the traditional pattern of the sovereign state continues unrestrained, responsible to no authority beyond its ruler's concept of the "national interest," these evolving weapons are likely to be used. They can be used for blackmail—"Give in or we'll let it loose"—as well as in actual combat.

In 1966 some 5,000 scientists, including 17 Nobelists, signed a petition to President Johnson in which they stated:

Chemical and biological weapons have the potential of inflicting, especially on civilians, enormous devastation and death, which may be unpredictable in scope and intensity. They could become far easier to produce than nuclear weapons . . . they lend themselves to use by leadership that may be desperate, irresponsible or unscrupulous. . . . United States forces have begun the large-scale use of anti-crop and "non-lethal" anti-personnel chemical weapons in Vietnam. We believe that this sets a dangerous precedent, with long-term hazards far outweighing any short-term military advantage.

The military establishment can be counted on to use any weapon, no matter how lethal, which seems to offer a chance of saving the homeland from humiliating surrender. American commanders detonated two atomic bombs over Japan with good conscience, though there is considerable evidence that Japan was ready to surrender without having to accept this terrible lesson. If Japan had had a couple of Polaris-carrying submarines at the moment, would she not have used them to obliterate Los Angeles and San Francisco? The question is academic. Would Nasser in the name of humanity have refrained from using nuclear weapons, or any biologicals and chemicals at his command, when the Israelis moved in on him on a June morning in 1967? Another academic question. A war generates strong fevers which defy rational behavior. Solemn commitments not to employ available weapons will, in a crisis, not be worth the paper they are written on. No sovereign state *in extremis* can be trusted to refrain from using its latest agent for annihilation.

A FEW NUCLEAR FACTS

The powers of nuclear bombs are now reasonably well established. To begin with, they are *not* comparable to TNT, the usual benchmark; they are in a new dimension altogether. They produce not one, but five, specific results, as follows:

1. A shock effect like that of TNT—up to one million times stronger.

2. A local heat effect of great destructiveness, that leaves an aftermath of blindness.

3. An immediate lethal radiation, drifting downwind.

4. A long-term fallout, circling the stratosphere and dangerous for years.

5. An exceedingly spectacular "firestorm" effect. It derives from an explosion high in the stratosphere and is capable of incinerating an area the size of Texas.

Secretary of Defense Robert S. McNamara testified in 1966 that in less than one hour of a full-scale nuclear attack, 100 million Americans would be killed. But, he continued, the United States could still retaliate from its hardened missile silos, and eliminate 100 million Russians, together with 80 percent of their industrial establishments. "Let me assure you," McNamara told the Armed Services Committee of the House, "that our strategic forces are sufficient to insure the destruction of both the Soviet Union and Communist China, under the worst imaginable circumstances."

The powers of nuclear weaponry are accepted by most scientists—especially the scientists who developed these powers— and by all intelligent laymen with a modicum of imagination. They are even formally acknowledged from time to time by chiefs of state, with the exception of Mao in China—who may not be as ignorant as his official pronouncements suggest. Sensible action by statesmen, based on the facts, however, is more uncertain, as the 20 years since Hiroshima have testified. Cultural lag is still powerful; witness the United States in Vietnam in 1967, taking much the same ideological stand that Theodore Roosevelt took in Cuba in 1898. American political leaders see a small country to be rescued from an aggressive tyrant, and a war to be won. On the other hand, the United States has officially recognized the constraints of the nuclear age by forbearing to overrun Cuba and so risk a thermonuclear duel with Russia.

A striking evaluation of the nuclear facts comes from Dr.

Jerome B. Wiesner and Dr. Herbert York, two outstanding American scientists. They said in 1964:

Both sides in the arms race are thus confronted by the dilemma of steadily increasing military power and steadily decreasing national security. It is our considered professional judgment that this dilemma has no technical solution. . . . The clearly predictable course of the arms race is a steady open spiral downward into oblivion.[1]

Nuclear physics has put this stunning paradox before the chiefs of state: *The more powerful a nation becomes, the more its national security diminishes.* As a corollary, Wiesner and York argue that no foreseeable weapons, either offensive or defensive, can upset the present standoff, or prevent mutual suicide if the buttons are actually pushed.

Chiefs of state, however, believe the scientists one day and disregard them the next. Indeed, it is hard to find a more convincing example of cultural lag than this convulsive return, on alternate days, to pre-nuclear power politics. Some of our leaders, political as well as military, stay there all the time. Gordon Harrison, reviewing General Nathan F. Twining's book *Neither Liberty nor Safety* in the *New York Times* of September 25, 1966, has this to say:

To read General Twining is to be transported out of the real world of complicated interrelationships among people and nations all having to be managed somehow under threat of a war that could cost several hundred million lives. One enters a fantasy world devised to meet the requirements of war games. . . . The art of surviving in this world is to have more of the better guns, and fewer scruples about using them whenever the odds favor your killing more on the enemy side than he can kill on yours. Military victory is always by definition the only final solution.

[1] *Scientific American,* October, 1964. Dr. Wiesner was President Kennedy's scientific adviser, now at MIT. Dr. York was scientific adviser to the Eisenhower Administration, now at the University of California.

To which Napoleon would certainly cry amen. But Wiesner and York, speaking for the world of today, see a spiral downward into oblivion.

OVERKILL AND DETERRENCE

The Napoleonic spirit seems still to determine foreign policy. Only the partial test ban of 1962, covering atomic explosions in the atmosphere, has registered a solid step in the direction of survival.

There are now, as I write, five members of the Nuclear Club, all in the business of manufacturing nuclear weapons and their delivery systems—the United States, Russia, Britain, France, and China. The first two have developed most of the technology, and are the major contestants in the arms race— "two scorpions in a bottle," Oppenheimer once called them. Both are responsible for the curious and ominous phenomenon of "overkill," which means more power of annihilation available than there are victims available—something altogether beyond Napoleon. A recent estimate indicated that the United States and Russia had enough in their nuclear stockpiles to allocate the equivalent of six tons of TNT, to say nothing of the other four effects of an atomic explosion, for every man, woman, and child on the planet.

The United States has perhaps five times as much overkill at hand as Russia, but in this curious encounter the United States derives no particular advantage. The Russians have enough to eliminate the United States, Europe, and China as viable societies—and what more do they need?

Here, indeed, is a strange spectacle for future historians— the ICBM's in their underground silos, ready to destroy three continents many times over. If a vigorous exchange really begins, the human condition retreats to the Stone Age. Protection by means of underground shelters has been pretty well discredited as overkill increases. How will the millions in Megalopolis have time to get into them?

But if the button is not pushed, these weapons act as deter-rents to war. No American President, or Russian chief of state, is particularly eager to eliminate his country. The Cuban missile crisis was much too close for comfort. Actually, of course, deterrence could be maintained equally well without the factor of overkill. Each side needs only enough to liqui-date the other side. This could be done by a fleet of nuclear submarines armed with Polaris or Poseidon missiles. If the United States retaliatory force is *only* ICBM's in the ground, says Dr. Ralph E. Lapp, the missiles must be launched *before* the silos are hit.[2] As long as submarines, however, can hide in the depth of the oceans, the decision to fire, he says, can be delayed until the facts of the crisis are better assessed and communicated from headquarters. ICBM's create a greater danger of war by accident than submarine missiles. Mean-while the dollar costs of maintaining deterrence can be enor-mously reduced. But this strategy would permit at the same time a very large reduction in overkill, a reduction which chiefs of state and their military advisers, to say nothing of the defense industries, seem to regard with great apprehension, as does the United States Congress. Even if defense is technically impossible, we are determined not to believe it.

THE ANTIMISSILE MISSILE

Many scientists as well as Wiesner and York are dubious about efforts to make defense draw level with offense in atomic warfare. One such project is a computer-directed atomic missile, which could be sent up by the defender to destroy enemy missiles before they zeroed in on "soft" targets (cities) or "hard" targets (ICBM silos).

In the first place there is doubt that such a missile could be effectively designed. It would have to be a very sophisticated weapon indeed to identify and demolish the real nuclear mis-sile among the shower of decoys that will be coming over at

[2] *Kill and Overkill,* Basic Books, 1963.

the same time. Can a computer detect a decoy? Again, the antimissile, detonating atomic bombs all over the home terrain, demands a huge fallout shelter program, especially for "soft" targets—that charming expression of the military for helpless city-dwellers. The total cost of the missile system and shelters to go with it is estimated at $30 to $40 billion, an amount rather more than the annual cost of the United States public school system.

In the third place, the antimissile missile is bound to exacerbate the arms race again, just when it was beginning to ease a little between the United States and Russia. Said James Reston: "McNamara fears that the project will develop a life of its own, and be expanded year after year, leading to new counterprograms by the Soviets." The antimissile psychology seems to be largely cultural lag. If we only spend enough, we can be made secure, we will win. Yet this attitude is as out of date as that of the Londoners who paraded to demand more Dreadnoughts before World War I:

> We want eight
> And we won't wait!

The antimissile defense system is further weakened by the new "multiple warhead." This technological triumph lets a single ICBM carry several bombs, aimed to hit not New York alone, but Boston, Philadelphia, Baltimore, and Washington as well.

PROLIFERATION AND ACCIDENT

As I write, these spirited proposals are still largely on paper. If deterrence is to deter, nuclear arms must be kept within the present five members of the club, with ironclad agreements carrying severe penalties. To secure such agreements from China is going to be no small task.

India and Pakistan have recently been at war over Kashmir, fighting with conventional arms, and India is now under pressure to build her own nuclear weapons. This she can do technically, and so can Egypt, Israel, Italy, Sweden, East Germany, Poland, Japan, Canada, Rumania—indeed, any nation which has a substantial industrial complex. While the peril goes up, costs come down as techniques are perfected. Furthermore, what is to prevent a small country arming itself by gift or purchase of missiles, bombs, and instructions from a club member? Castro, we remember, hoped to do this in Cuba. Proliferation, unless halted by a very rugged agreement, is likely to speed up as the Hungry World grows more crowded and hungrier. The developing nations, frustrated and desperate from overpopulation, may try nuclear blackmail.

Even if proliferation can be stopped, even if deterrence can somehow be indefinitely maintained, the peril of *accident* remains. It can occur at any time, anywhere, due to man failure or machine failure, or both. When a great nation is tooled up to deliver an avalanche of destruction at 15 million degrees Centigrade in less than an hour's time, the network of electronic, mechanical, chemical, and semantic signal systems is very formidable. One does not have to sit in a corner room in the Pentagon to understand this. A good many things can go wrong. Several signals in the United States defense network have already been tripped by accident, once by a flight of gulls. Then there was the crash of four United States hydrogen bombs from a plane on the Spanish coast. Enough radioactivity seeped out to poison the earth around the village of Palomares, and acres of soil had to be dug up and removed. "The danger of more and more tragic accidents," says the *New York Times,* "is bound to increase with the entry of each additional nation into the nuclear club."

War began in hand-to-hand fighting with clubs and sticks. When the bow was invented, battle lines could be pulled back, at least until the final rush. When the musket was invented, lines could be further separated in combat. A soldier need not see the face of his enemy. He fired, as Kipling said, "into the brown of them." In nuclear war no battle lines at all remain. Combat is by remote control, up to half a world away. A circuit is closed, and within a few minutes 200 million civilians die.

THE COLLISION COURSE

The above facts about the arms race are only a small sample of those now solidly on the record. Why then do our political leaders, encouraged by most of us citizens, continue on a collision course? Because the Russians do? Why do the Russians continue?

There appear to be several deeply rooted reasons for both sides to continue. One is what psychologists call *denial*. Another is the limited nature of human comprehension, including the perception of time. Another is the nature of the sovereign state, which intensifies the "we versus they" principle, and gives its leaders a paramount responsibility for military defense. Another is the tendency to fear an adversary rather than a process, so that we concentrate on the *balance* in a given situation rather than on the terror below. If we are *even* with Russia, we can relax, although she is quite capable of blowing us to kingdom come, and vice versa. The Russians can relax if they feel that they are even with America.

Perhaps the strongest reason why we do not change the collision course is the fact that we are culture-bound, locked in prenuclear habits. The collective patterns which should assure our survival, with all their ancient traditions reinforced by natural selection down the ages, *are now working against survival*. Unless we realize the danger in this situation—a danger in ourselves as well as in our weapons—the future is dubious indeed.

Let us look a little more closely at some of the factors which now block survival.

DENIAL

By denial psychologists, such as Dr. Jerome Frank of Johns Hopkins, mean a rejection of difficult problems and seemingly remote dangers. Mothers of small children are alarmed about fallout in milk, which only mildly excites the rest of us. But 100 million dead . . . "Who's pitching for the Dodgers this afternoon?" Baseball is not the only avenue of escape. Some of us, indeed a great many of us, watch TV; some look at the stars; some titillate their credulity with flying saucers. Some concentrate on art or on music, whether Bach or rock 'n' roll. Yet the more we repress these fears, the deeper they lurk in the unconscious mind, to contribute to the growing mood of alienation, particularly in young people.

LIMITS OF COMPREHENSION

Next, regard the limitation of our human faculties in coping with large figures. I confess it very difficult for me to conceive of half the people in America lying contorted and silent. I think of one or two bad highway accidents I have seen, but even more I remember areas ruined by erosion, forest fire, or strip mining. I remember the utter desolation spread by the fumes of a copper smelter in Ducktown, Tennessee. Spread such devastation over the whole country, compound it with radiation that prevents green foliage from coming back for decades if not forever, and I can picture a land without life, a land on which any people who survived would not want to live.

Here is one facet of the puzzle: how can the incontrovertible facts of a thermonuclear exchange be made credible without paralyzing the hearer's sensitivity? The trouble is not with the validity of the facts, or even their static acceptance by the mind; the trouble lies in how to make the acceptance dynamic, so that people feel it in their bones, and demand counteraction.

Some distinguished physical scientists have been concerned with this problem. It is partly a matter of semantics, of communication. Here is Dr. Frank Oppenheimer, (brother of the late Robert Oppenheimer), professor of physics at the University of Colorado. The bomb, he says in the *Saturday Review,* has been called "brighter than a thousand suns," but what does multiplying or dividing by a factor of 1,000 really mean? He asks us to try it in some personal situations. If your income of $9,000 is scaled down by a factor of 1,000 you would be left with $9 a year to support the family. That registers all right. Again, there are now 12,000 students in your alma mater, let us say. Multiplied by 1,000 the campus would have to accommodate 12 million youngsters under the elms. That registers, too.

During World War II, Dr. Oppenheimer continues, the largest single airplane load of explosives was about 10 tons of TNT. Today, a single ICBM warhead can carry the equivalent of 10 *million* tons of TNT. Such facts are known but are held on the threshold of the mind. Most changes we deal with involve an increase factor of less than 100 times. World population, for all its ominous portent, is still only eight times as large as it was in 1650. A jet airliner travels only about 100 times as fast as man can walk. A factor of 100 we can perhaps deal with, but a million often might as well be a billion or a trillion.

Dr. Albert Szent-Gyorgi (St. George to Americans), Nobel Prize scientist, develops this thought.[3] The characteristics and the nervous system of Homo sapiens, he says, were evolved over the aeons. They enabled him to live in an environment of land and water, where he needed no microscopes, telescopes, Geiger counters, or radar to bring up the family and survive.

[3] *Science, Ethics and Politics,* Vanguard, 1964.

We are not adapted to the submicroscopic realities of the atom; they are too explosive and too fast. None of our built-in reactions can cope with them. Indeed, they are not coping any too well with highway travel at a mere 70 miles an hour. We are accordingly, says Szent-Gyorgi, very vulnerable to what technology has let loose in the world since 1945.

The best hope, he says, is to make one's mind realize that the very large and the very small can both put us in great jeopardy. It should not be too difficult for normal minds to conclude that 15 million degrees Centigrade, the heat in an exploding nuclear bomb, is not something their political leaders can fool around with. The diplomatic footwork of the 1930's is no longer adequate for the foreign policy of the 1960's. This thought one can seize, even if all the zeros escape comprehension.

John von Neumann, that extraordinary mathematician who helped make the computer possible, offers a revealing analogy to help us comprehend nuclear power. A big war today, he says, would be like confining a war in the year 1900 to Manhattan Island in New York, using the weapons of that time. Manhattan is 15 miles by 2, and we had 13-inch naval guns in 1900, capable of sending an explosive shell at least 20 miles. The world is much too small for the use of modern weapons. Professor Platt carries the point farther when he says that "the world has now become too dangerous for anything less than Utopia."

In coping with distances beyond our direct perception, we depend on a process of abstracting, where our ordinary evaluations do not hold. This helps to explain why human beings lack certain inhibitions possessed by most animals, including the tendency to avoid unnecessary conflict. Konrad Lorenz says that man's trouble

arises from his being a basically harmless, omnivorous creature, lacking in natural weapons with which to kill big prey, and, therefore, also devoid of the built-in safety devices which prevent big carnivores from abusing their killing power to destroy members of their own species. . . . In human evolution, no inhibitory mechanisms preventing sudden manslaughter were necessary, because quick killing was impossible anyhow; the potential victim had plenty of opportunity to elicit pity from the aggressor . . . until, all of a sudden, the invention of artificial weapons upset the equilibrium. . . . The distance at which all shooting weapons take effect screens the killer . . . the deep, emotional layers of our personality simply do not register the fact that the crooking of the forefinger to release a shot tears the entrails of another man.[4]

When the forefinger is transferred to a switch releasing a warhead to be detonated 10,000 miles away, the personality registers even less. What Lorenz is saying is that a lion or a tiger has an instinctive genetic protection against mutual suicide with which Homo sapiens unfortunately is not blessed.

Albert Wohlstetter, another distinguished scientist, warns that with nuclear weapons and their delivery systems "we have run up against earth's finite limits." Missiles can reach any point on the globe in a few minutes, and the area of devastation for unhardened (i.e., "soft") targets is very large in relation to the accuracy of delivery. This means that potential destruction is close to 100 percent.

Wohlstetter is dubious, moreover, about using probability theory in the technical sense to estimate a future thermonuclear exchange. There is no experience on which to base the calculation. "The argument for the statistical certainty of nuclear war should be no more terrifying than the argument for the statistical certainty of eternal peace is reassuring."[5] The only safety we are permitted to contemplate is relative.

FINALLY

Does the reader remember the popular cartoon in the newspapers and weekly magazines showing the atomic bomb

---

[4] *On Aggression,* Harcourt, Brace & World, 1966.
[5] *Bulletin of the Atomic Scientists,* October, 1964.

as something like a fat alderman with little pig eyes and a most sinister expression? We seldom see him nowadays. But he is still around, with no change for the better in his expression. Deterrence has held for 20 years, with some intelligent guidance and a good deal of luck in avoiding accidents. So most people have been fortified in their exercise of denial.

I would not be an honest reporter of technological trends if I did not try to document a condition which is still deadly serious. Today, however, it is not so much war between the United States and Russia which is the chief danger as the proliferation of nuclear weapons to other nations. Only close collaboration between the two great superpowers can halt this.

12

NATIONALISM—WHICH WAY?

NATIONALISM today is characterized by a curious ambivalence; it is both gaining and ebbing. Since World War II there has been a veritable deluge of new sovereign states. When the United Nations was founded in 1945, there were 50 flags in the plaza; at the beginning of 1967 there were 122—causing U Thant to ask a limit to the creation of any more "microstates." It is reasonable to suppose that "rising expectations" for a better life hastened the disintegration of the British, French, and Dutch empires.

At the same time, technology has been welding the nations, new and old, ever more firmly together, breaking down frontiers and barriers which once separated them. Transportation and communication, especially air traffic and communications satellites, are revolutionizing traditional boundary lines.

In this chapter we will explore both trends. They represent something so new in the world that our exploration will have to be tentative. The historians have not yet got around to any definite examination of what is happening politically to the Congo, to North Korea, or to Barbados.

WHAT IS A NATION?

The small island of Barbados in the West Indies—166 square miles, population 242,000—was released in 1966 from what remains of the British Empire, to become a sovereign state. The Union Jack was run down, and the new national flag of ultramarine and gold run up, before a cheering crowd. A few days later the flag joined the 121 other flags on the plaza in front of the United Nations in New York.

A "nation" today is not a culture, not a language, a race, a religion, or even a contiguous territory—look at Pakistan, east and west. Nations have taken many political forms since the first city-states arose 5,000 years ago. They have been governed by high priests, kings, emperors, dictators, juntas, generals, holy men, presidents, parliaments, privy councils— modified from time to time by leagues and alliances. They have attached and detached groups of colonies. Ever since the Treaty of Westphalia, however, which ended the Thirty Years' War between Protestants and Catholics in 1648, a sovereign state has embraced a number of common characteristics, including:

The power of life or death over its citizens, mitigated by some system of law, courts, and police.
A military establishment for defense of its territory—and recently its air space.
An economic establishment for coining local money, raising taxes, setting up conditions for agriculture, industry, and trade with other nations. A mint and a customhouse come early.
A diplomatic establishment for dealing with other states.
A flag, a national anthem, and an account of past heroes and glorious traditions, to be taught in the home and in the schools.

When she was released from the British Empire, India promptly adopted all of the above, with Mahatma Gandhi as her outstanding hero. How far Barbados will go toward establishing an army and a currency remains to be seen; she will no doubt aspire to both.

Since the Treaty of Westphalia it has been pretty well agreed that a sovereign state is the sole judge of its national interest, and can proceed unilaterally to do whatever it has the military and economic power to do. "World opinion" may frown—but what can world opinion do? In theory, all nations possess absolute sovereignty, beyond and above any international rules, laws, or agreements. The Nuremberg Trials, where members of the Nazi Party in Germany were formally charged with high crimes against mankind, were a sobering example of the uncertainty of a rule of law superior to national sovereignty. Many jurists arose to ask: "By what right can the German Government be judged, beyond the right of military conquest?" Others raised the embarrassing question: "Suppose comparable charges had been brought against the United States for the nuclear bombing of Hiroshima, would she have accepted prison terms for her generals?"

Down the years, various nations have suddenly appeared, like the United States in the late eighteenth century, India in 1946, little Barbados in 1966; and nations have disappeared, like Poland, to reappear again; like Estonia, which is still without a flag. Nations have enormously expanded, like Russia, and have surprisingly shrunk, like Austria and Japan. But the characteristics of sovereignty—the flag, the army, the diplomats, and the currency, as well as the fierce loyalty—have endured.

"Nationalism," says historian Herbert J. Muller, "is not just human nature. Although it derives from age-old tribalism, the impassioned devotion to the nation-state is a recent development, and a distinctively Western one. . . . Now it has swept all over the world, to give the West plenty of trouble."

The thermonuclear bomb, and the obliteration of frontiers due to air power and orbiting in space, are combining to forge new patterns. NATO, for instance, was set up after the war to prevent the sweep of Russian land armies and tanks into Western Europe. Is there anyone left who is so naïve as to believe that such a sweep would be a practical military operation in the era of ICBM's and jet bombers? Again, Russia, within her land masses, and America, between her two oceans, were once well protected. Where are those natural defenses now?

DEGREES OF SOVEREIGNTY

There is a progression from absolute national sovereignty, to internationalism, and then on to supranationalism. At the far end of the scale, a state with no sovereign rights at all, just a parcel of land within a comprehensive world government, would cease to be a nation. Is this the end of the trend curve which modern states are riding? Possibly, but I very much doubt it.

Now let us move back on the scale and consider *internationalism*. It is a loose term, but we can define it somewhat arbitrarily as a stage where the several states, still largely sovereign, agree to handle certain functions—such as the mails or the fisheries—in cooperation with other states. The Common Market of six European countries is a notable example of international agreement today.

At this stage, any nation can, theoretically at least, denounce its treaties, pacts, and agreements, if it feels its national interest threatened. Indonesia walks out of the United Nations, which is still largely in the international frame, and what can anybody do about it? Then she walks in again.

When the links which technology is forging grow so strong that a nation hesitates to sever them, that nation can be ready to enter a compact which it will not, or cannot, denounce. Such a compact normally calls for a superagency to inspect and administer the provisions of the agreement; an agency beyond and above the control of any one state. We may call this an example of *supranationalism*. The management of Antarctica, following the treaty between 12 nations in 1959, is a supranational undertaking. So is the Atomic Test Ban Treaty of 1963. If and when a substantial reduction in armaments is agreed to, an inspection agency organized with penalties set, supranationalism will really come into its own. Internationalism can be expressed: "We'll do it if all goes well," and supranationalism: "We've jolly well got to do it."

GROWING INTERDEPENDENCE

In 1700 many towns in America could supply most of their economic needs from inside their own boundaries. Food was locally grown, shelter was built by hand, clothing was spun, woven, and fabricated. By 1900 these handicrafts had mostly disappeared in favor of products brought in by rail or stage from all over the United States. No town could survive for long without such imports. What the economists called the economy of scarcity had surrendered to the economy of abundance.

Today, in the 1960's, economic interdependence has spread to the whole planet. No nation, not even the U.S. or the U.S.S.R., can function without materials and services from other countries. There are very few self-sufficient tribes left for anthropologists to study. The so-called Hungry World, as we noted earlier, stands in dire need not only of food imports, raw materials, and machinery, but of birth control clinics as well. All countries are now concerned with electronic communication, air transport, weather reports, and the effects of radioactive fallout.

THE COMMON MARKET

To administer this growing interdependence the several nations have established agreements in the domain of both internationalism and supranationalism, as we have tried to define them. To my mind, none is more significant than the Common Market of Europe, to which France, Germany, Italy, Belgium, the Netherlands, and Luxembourg subscribe. Britain will probably come in, and other European nations as well. The idea is to reduce economic wastes arising from tariff barriers and destructive competition, and to establish a continental free market something akin to that of the United States.

Beyond the Common Market lies the idea of what is sometimes called the "Third Force," a kind of United States of Europe. This could be a very formidable political, economic, and military arrangement. In the Olympic Games of 1966 in Japan, the U.S. won 36 gold medals, Russia won 30, but Europe, outside of Russia, won 68—with silver and bronze medals in proportion. Russia and the United States have literate populations of approximately 200 million each, while Western Europe has 350 million. It has 75 million tons of shipping in its merchant fleets against 23 million for the U.S. In 1962 Europe produced 100 million tons of steel, the U.S. 89 million.

Thus the "Third Force" can stand right up to the U.S., and readily overpower the U.S.S.R., in both population and production. It has a better faculty in the pure sciences, if not in technology, more skilled workers, fewer disruptions due to automation, and a good deal more sense about money and credit. Europe understands Keynesian economics, and is further along in the march toward a mixed economy.

There is as yet no political union, and many bitter national hatreds remain in Europe. But if the various states, including the fringe along the decaying Iron Curtain, ever do form a supranational political union, they might well become the dominant economic and scientific power in the world. I refrain from adding military, for there can be no truly dominant military power in an age of overkill and mutual suicide.

A historic transformation is under way, not only within Europe, but in Europe's relations with the world. It continues—despite General de Gaulle's ambitions, Britain's confusions, Moscow's opposition and Washington's distraction in Asia—because it responds profoundly to the needs of the times in politics as well as economics.

Thus in 1966 the *New York Times* looks along the trend curve of the Common Market. As I write, a common market for Latin America is being seriously discussed by members of the Organization of American States.

The technological imperative is eroding national frontiers on the one hand and encouraging regionalism on the other. Regionalism is growing in Latin America not only for a common market, but for an area free from atomic weapons. Eastern Europe is also agitating for such an area by virtue of the famous Rapacki Plan. New nations in Africa have a loose and belligerent regional organization. It is probable that regionalism will be increasingly relied upon to complement and stabilize the inadequate economies of the member states. It will also, of course, further weaken the principle of national sovereignty.

ACROSS FRONTIERS

Apart from regional groupings, the sheer impact of applied science grows continually, with profound effects on people around the world. Examples have been cited and here is a brief summary:

> The mounting air traffic between nations.
> Radio and television; Telstar as a world agency.
> Moving pictures, especially American films. Per contra, European films are now coming into America in volume.
> Weather reports, vital to air and ocean traffic.
> Computerized information for ocean traffic. Take the case of the injured sailor, described in Chapter 9.
> The "hot line" from the U.S. to the U.S.S.R.

The above effects can be classified as useful; here are some penetrations of a different order:

Fallout from bomb tests, now perpetrated by France and China and probably doing lasting injury to the human pool of genes.
U-2 spying planes. They are usually too high to be shot down, and so can fly into the air space of any nation—and do.
Atomic submarines, capable of hugging a coast undetected.
The ugly possibility of missiles on space platforms in orbit.
Air pollution from industry and motor vehicles, wafted across frontiers. The nations of Europe are especially vulnerable.
Water pollution across frontiers—the Great Lakes, the Danube, the Rhine.

Thus, whether the impact of science is benign as in the case of the Common Market, or malignant, as in the case of fallout, or ambivalent as in the case of exported American films, national frontiers are penetrated, and the classical concept of sovereignty undermined.

Technology in the form of gunpowder made the armored knight obsolete. Cervantes wrote an epitaph for feudalism in *Don Quixote.* Now the sovereign state seems in equal jeopardy, and from a parallel cause—except that the explosives are far more potent. Who shall write the epitaph of the national state? Perhaps the nuclear physicists who contribute to the *Bulletin of the Atomic Scientists* are writing an introduction.

THE RISING EPIDEMIC OF NATIONALISM

The curious paradox, however, remains: even as frontiers are increasingly breached, more than 50 new nations are now on the map, all aspiring to the standard characteristics of nationalism—flag, anthem, police power, army, currency; all duly entitled to a 21-gun salute when the chief of state pays a visit to Washington.

The trend curve indicates that the Portuguese Empire will presently follow the pattern and add half a dozen more independent states. Interestingly enough, Portugal, the last of the empires, has the lowest standard of living in Western Europe.

The new nations are mostly in what we have called the Hungry World, where population is outrunning its nutrients. They aspire to be political democracies, but their economies are extremely vulnerable, as noted. One after another, their civilian presidents have been exiled if not assassinated, to be followed by a military dictator or junta—a procedure long familiar in Latin America. No social scientist should be surprised by this sequence, for the reason is plain: *the new nations have no substantial middle class.* Without a middle class political democracy is unworkable. Citizens of the Hungry World are mostly poor peasants with a few wealthy landowners on top—as in South Vietnam. Democracy cannot function in such a climate.

Again, the new nations have few trained civil servants, without whom a stable government is impossible. When the Belgian Congo won its independence, there were said to be fewer than a dozen natives with college education. Tribesmen, however innately intelligent, cannot be expected to operate a modern state without a lot of training.

Again, while the price of manufactured articles tends to increase in high-energy societies, the price of raw materials— cotton, copra, coffee—tends to remain stationary or decline in low-energy societies. Many of the new nations receive less for their exports, and pay more for their imports, than before independence. To make matters worse, affluent societies have substantial R & D programs for the invention and manufacture of more and more synthetics—plastics, rubber, textiles such as nylon. This tends to reduce their imports of natural products from the ex-colonies.

Again, with the world in its present condition of explosive

change, private investors are not eager to sink their capital in a country which may have a revolution tomorrow morning and which may expropriate all foreign holdings. Nor are they eager to sink their capital in Africa, south of the Sahara, where racial and tribal tensions hover on the edge of violence.

Colonialism in Africa reduced hundreds of autonomous tribes, kingdoms, petty states, to some 50 colonies. Most of these have now become "sovereign nations."[1] But 50 is a ridiculously large number. What is the chance for economic and industrial growth when nations are as small as this? "The overriding need is for effective *regional* development and planning." In the seven years from 1960 to 1967 there were 22 coups in Africa, some bloody and violent.

Mr. Morris Janowitz, writing in the *Bulletin of the Atomic Scientists,* hoped to find a new nation without a military establishment and its attendant drain on the national budget. He was disappointed; even tiny Togo had her soldiers. "It appears to be a universal political conception," he says "that a new state requires an army. . . . Investment in the military is a fundamental cost which new nations are prepared to invest, whatever the economic ability to pay."

The *Economist* reported in early 1967 that little Somalia in Africa, with a population of 2.5 million poor peasants, supports an army of 25,000. It is said to have recently received from the Soviet Union 150 MIG fighter planes, 20 helicopters, and enough T-34 tanks to form an armored brigade. The poor peasants will have to scratch their arid fields even harder.

No matter how competent the surviving dictator, most of the nations carved out of the British, French, and Dutch empires are not self-supporting viable societies. Not all observers are yet prepared to admit this, but who can deny it? It is safe

[1] Colin Legum of the London *Observer* in *Current,* August, 1967.

to assume that the brood from the Portuguese Empire will be
no sturdier. These six reasons have been set forth:

1. Population outrunning food production
2. No stabilizing middle class
3. Inadequately trained administrators
4. High military budgets
5. Lower prices for local raw materials, higher prices for
manufactured imports
6. Hesitant investors from the affluent world

From the standpoint of economics, historian Henry Steele
Commager has well said, "Nationalism has passed its merid-
ian," as outmoded as "states' rights" in America.

Against these six handicaps it is difficult to see how a number of these nations can long endure. They may wither as
suddenly as they blossomed.

All these newspaper maps which divide the world into Communist and non-Communist, developed and underdeveloped countries, should add a third category, especially for Southeast Asia—
ephemeral.[2]

Where can they go, these ephemeral nations; what is their
political future? Can colonialism come back and reabsorb
them? No, it is too late—though there has been a slight effort
in that direction by Belgium in the Congo. Colonialism uprooted the tribal patterns which had established viable cultures
in much of Africa and Asia. Then, after stripping the area of
its easily exploitable resources, colonialism left no alternate
patterns for carrying on. There the ex-colonies are, between
the devil and the deep sea.

It seems only just and reasonable that the affluent societies
which destroyed them should now return, not to rule them,
but to help them in massive programs of rehabilitation and
population control. It would seem better for such programs to

[2] Arthur Bonner in a letter to *New York Times.*

be administered by the United Nations, or other supranational agency, rather than by jealous states looking, as they usually do, for ideological, military, and political advantage.

Beyond keeping the Hungry World viable—which must be a major objective in the years immediately before us—one can glimpse the possibility of regional alliances to provide an economic stability that the new nations lack as separate units. Also, substantial help should come from the development of cheap atomic energy, as outlined in Chapter 7.

The Common Market may be evolving into a model for regionalism. Could the new nations form a Southeast Asia federation, an economic alliance in North Africa, in East Africa, West Africa, the Caribbean? Uncertain as such political development may seem, where else can Barbados, Vietnam, and Sierra Leone go?

The 13 American colonies once broke away from the imperial rule of Britain to form a regional federation, which was unified by the Constitution of 1787. In due course it spread over a continental area. Connecticut, or Georgia, by itself made little economic sense, even in 1787, and, despite the vociferous advocates of states' rights, neither makes any sense at all as a sovereign state today.

IN CONCLUSION

For the short term, the status of the new nations in Asia, Africa, and the Caribbean is unstable if not ephemeral. Nationalism is gaining no dependable victories in this area, despite the growing number of flags in the plaza of the United Nations.

For the longer term, nationalism as we have known it for 300 years is also inoperable for well-established high-energy societies, as technology dissolves their frontiers. The Common Market, the Organization of American States, the Nuclear Club, the *détente* between Russia and the U.S., the United

Nations, are all eroding the legacy of Westphalia.

From nationalism to regionalism, to internationalism, supranationalism, the United Nations, the World Court, finally to genuine world government—at least for disarmament and other mandatory functions—this seems to be the political trend, if Armageddon does not intervene. The paradox cited at the beginning of this chapter—increasing interdependence together with an epidemic of nationalism—may turn out to be brief.

The only road for all nations to follow, in the face of the technological imperative, would seem to be toward some kind of enforceable world order. In the next chapter we will try to appraise this trend, the last of the ten.

★

13.

ONE WORLD

THE TREND toward peace is strong, but the curve is jagged. No sooner do we get the Test Ban Treaty than fighting erupts in Vietnam. Intelligent leaders realize the appalling danger of such fighting but seem unable to rise above their built-in, prenuclear habits. Some people attribute these lapses to an ineradicable flaw in human nature, but such a conclusion leads straight to the "spiral into oblivion." Social scientists have a better explanation in the phenomenon of cultural lag. We act the way we were brought up to act and it is hard to change, regardless of reason and logic. This is what Toynbee meant when he said: "We shall have a hard struggle with ourselves to save ourselves from ourselves."

A QUESTION OF PRIORITIES

Ever since the publication of his book *The Martial Spirit,* Walter Millis has been recognized as an outstanding student of the twin trends toward war and peace. In a recent book, *An End to Arms,* he projects the latter curve some years into the future, and gives us some solid grounds for hope. He carefully avoids predicting a Utopia, and confines himself to forecasting a definite trend, based on the recent past. This is also my objective.

Peace and disarmament we must have, says Millis, but *how*

do we get from here to there? He detects some advance since 1954, the year which followed the death of Stalin. Nuclear weapons, though they have been multiplied and made more lethal, have nowhere been used. Deterrence has held, and he thinks it is gradually undermining the assumptions of the traditional war system. No technological breakthrough has occurred to challenge the overwhelming lead of offensive weapons. (Scientists Wiesner and York concur, as noted earlier.)

Russia has withdrawn her armed forces from Austria, and Antarctica has come under supranational control, with the U.S. and the U.S.S.R. cooperating in the agreement. The Cuban crisis taught a stunning lesson to both the great nuclear powers. Meanwhile "Communism" as a monolithic political entity, which had some validity under Stalin, is now split into a series of nationalistic states, with Peking denouncing Moscow even more vigorously than it denounces Washington. As a result, says Millis, "Since neither the Soviet nor Western power centers could any longer hope to take over the dominance of the world, co-existence became unavoidable."

Observe that he does not say that coexistence is something to hope for and work for; he says it is *unavoidable*. If he is right, and I believe he is, we have made an important advance on the road to peace since Stalin died. Moscow, confronted with the "unavoidable," has been logical enough to revise Lenin's theory of world revolution, with its anticipated world wars, and to substitute the doctrine of coexistence between East and West, where nuclear wars are abandoned in favor of less deadly forms of competition.

The division of the planet into "capitalist" and "Communist" states, accepted by both Stalin and John Foster Dulles, has now hopelessly collapsed. Millis expects the discrepancy to continue. He envisions two kinds of disputes in the years immediately ahead. First, we may expect serious quarrels be-

tween nations, where both parties sedulously avoid the resort
to conventional weapons, realizing that such preliminary violence is extremely likely to escalate into all-out nuclear war.
The crises over the Berlin corridor and the Formosa Straits
are examples. In prenuclear times either dispute would have
erupted into a big war. Second, we may expect limited en-
counters with conventional weapons, where escalation to
World War III is possible but not probable. Vietnam, Israel,
and Kashmir are examples.

As these crises and frustrations continue, the several military establishments will gradually decline into national police
forces; they no longer have a useful function against other
nations. The case for disarmament will be advanced by the
logic of events. Nations will ask why they should tax themselves for a vast, dangerous, and costly military establishment
which has nowhere to go except to its own destruction. What
price overkill?

International conferences that are called for general disarmament today, Millis warns, are likely to be unproductive if
not futile. They put the cart before the horse: *the priorities are
reversed*. We must, he says, have some dependable machinery
for settling disputes *before* disarmament proposals can make
significant headway. How right he is. What sovereign state is
going to disarm unilaterally if there is no acceptable way to
defend its interests? "It is not primarily a question of defang-
ing the war system, but the much more creative one of how to
make positive use of the possibilities that a demilitarized world
would open up." Something in the nature of $130 billion a
year would go far to promote these possibilities—the amount
spent in 1966 for armaments around the world, according to
the United Nations. ($145 billion is estimated for 1967.)

What would the machinery for settling disputes look like?
Many students of the problem, as well as Millis, identify three
cardinal factors:

1. A body of supranational law, including as a minimum prohibitions against armed aggression and the maintenance of aggressive weapons.

2. A system of World Courts to apply the law.

3. A supranational police force to see that the regulations are observed. Clark and Sohn in their *World Peace Through World Law* add a fourth factor: a World Development Authority.

Millis believes we should begin with the most pressing problem—the threat of nuclear war, including the proliferation of nuclear weapons. If this can be controlled, disarmament itself becomes "unavoidable." Tensions can then gradually relax, affording a breathing space for the next step toward an orderly world.

The United Nations and its affiliates are already beginning to move in this general direction. True, the body of law has only progressed to a series of resolutions following lengthy debate, but there is a functioning World Court to which cases are occasionally referred, and a police force which, when it can be financed, helps to keep the peace, as in Cyprus and the Congo.

A ROSTER OF INTERNATIONAL AGENCIES

In addition to the UN and its affiliates, many agencies are operating to unite the peoples of the world—some international, as defined earlier, some supranational. In 1965 the total number, including the UN group, was almost two thousand—to be exact, 1,897. Some agencies are small and weak, some huge and powerful. Some are regional, others worldwide. All are described at length—their inaugural dates, their goals, their officers, budgets, accomplishments—in a *Year Book,* published by the Union of International Agencies in Brussels, which runs to more than a thousand pages. First come the UN affiliates, an impressive list, including:

The World Court, the protoype of the judicial system which is to come

The World Bank, now very much in business, loaning large sums for hydroelectric systems and other capital improvements

The International Monetary Fund, for stabilizing national currencies—the dollar, the pound, the franc

The International Development Agency (IDA) helping the under-developed world with non-interest-bearing credits, carefully allocated

The International Labor Organization (ILO), the trade union international, founded in 1919

The International Civil Aviation Organization, to coordinate and safeguard the airways of the world, an increasingly vital task of supranationalism

The International Maritime Organization, for safety at sea

The Tariff and Trade Agency (GATT), to coordinate and liberalize tariffs

The World Meteorological Organization, for world weather studies and reports, conducting the World Meteorological Year

The International Atomic Energy Agency, to develop peaceful uses of the atom in generating power, in medicine, industry, agriculture

The Brussels *Year Book* lists and describes the agencies which are seeking to unify Europe—that "Third Force" out-lined in the last chapter. There are more than one hundred of them, beginning with the Common Market. Some of these regional organizations may be, of course, pressure groups for the nations in the region, rather than ambassadors for world peace; but all tend to undermine the concept of absolute na-tional sovereignty.

Next in the *Year Book* come 150 intergovernmental organ-izations, also undermining exclusive nationalism. They in-clude NATO, OAS (the Organization of American States), the Warsaw Pact, Benelux, and various Asian and African groups . . . all the way down to the "Administrative Center of Social Security for Rhine Boatmen," and the "Union for the Protection of New Varieties of Plants."

We note various international agencies concerned with the law, with the professions, with employers, with economic and financial groups, commerce, manufacturing, agriculture, transport and travel agencies, technical and scientific groups, health and social welfare. Here one finds the Red Cross and the International Planned Parenthood Association. Particularly significant to my mind are the scientific societies. Science is by definition knowledge open to all mankind, and these societies are often in a running battle with national governments to maintain free exchange of scientific data.

The informal "Pugwash Conferences," mentioned earlier, strikingly illustrate supranational concerns. Scientists worried about nuclear problems come from all over the world—from Russia, the U.S., Canada, Britain, India, Japan, Eastern and Western Europe—from both sides of the Iron Curtain. In 1960 there was a delegation from mainland China. The 1966 Pugwash meeting was held in Poland, the 1967 meeting in Sweden. The scientists gather as responsible citizens of the world, not as representatives of any nation, race, or creed. They try to focus the scientific method on such urgent problems as arms limitation, inspection systems, the reduction of tensions, how to strengthen the United Nations. These meetings are unique in world history.

One notes also the world-wide advance in fusion power—that variety of inanimate energy which promises to last indefinitely. Fusion research was declassified by all nations in 1958. Says the *Scientific American* (December, 1966): "Progress has been impressive in many laboratories around the world. We now have a vigorous new technology and new basic knowledge that is already influential not only in fusion research but also in astrophysics, space research and many other areas."

The *Year Book* describes international sports—which can be highly competitive, and so a substitute for shot and shell—including the Olympic Games, the great ISF (ski) races, Davis Cup tennis. It describes international organizations concerned with ethics, religion, education, the social sciences, literature, and the arts. Here, too, an author finds the international patent and copyright agencies which seek to protect creative artists and inventors.

Some of the 1,897 organizations are obviously Utopian; some are oriented to a region, an industry, or an ideology. But as one studies the *Year Book,* most agencies seem essentially practical, set up to meet a human need which could not be met by a single nation. Take, for instance, the convention signed by 29 countries in London in July, 1965 in which merchant fleets, representing three-quarters of the world's tonnage, agreed not to dump oil wastes into the sea within 50 miles of any coastline.

As applied science overrides national frontiers, the need to control its impact increases. Sooner or later the pressure builds up in a given field to become so severe that steps are taken—almost two thousand steps to date, according to the *Year Book.* We *had* to set up a world-wide postal service; we *had* to devise international controls for epidemics and plant diseases; we *had* to issue rules for safety at sea; to distribute weather reports for planes and ships on all the oceans; to control cables, radio telephones, and now Telstar.

By 1968 no inhabited place on earth will be out of range for Telstar with its transmission by telephone, radio, television. Even if the villagers do not comprehend the message, some visiting anthropologist is likely to pass it along. Consider what this opens up in the way of instant communication to the last person on earth. Consider the stark necessity of keeping political and ideological propaganda off the airwaves. UNESCO is already working on a program for world-wide education, via what someone has called an "electronic blackboard," beamed by a satellite into the schoolroom.

WHO OWNS THE MOON?

Technology is forcing us not only beyond the traditional rights of individual property owners, but beyond the legal domain of sovereign states. Who owns the moon, Mars, the solar system? What are the rules for free movement in outer space? Who has title to the hydrogen of the oceans, someday the source of fusion power? Who owns the wealth at the bottom of the seas and the minerals in the earth's mantle? Who has the right to bring a meteorite, consisting of pure iron, to Pittsburgh or the Ruhr for steelmaking?

Such questions demand a planetary code of law, with recourse to the World Court. A subcommittee of the United Nations, at work on a blueprint for space law, is considering such matters as liability for damages caused by "space objects," freedom for exploration in space by all nations, assistance to astronauts who may come down on foreign territory, and the like. The American Bar Association, under the able leadership of Charles S. Rhyne, is also drafting a code, in cooperation with lawyers in other countries.

Radioactive fallout is blown around the world, and, if the wind is adverse, can damage a neutral country as severely as a belligerent in a thermonuclear exchange.

Some kind of weather control, for all its dangers, is on the trend curve. Who gets the rain, the dry spells, the high winds, and the fine days for harvesting? The allocation of rainfall may be the toughest problem in weather control, but perhaps it can be mitigated somewhat by desalting sea water in great nuclear plants. Then who gets the radioactive wastes?

Even a brief study of the *Year Book* lifts one mentally out of his own backyard, and shows him, as from a mountaintop, the network of functional demands and agencies linking all nations and all peoples. Beyond those already in operation, one can envision from this high point the agencies which are to come—enforcing the law for outer space and for the riches of the oceans; directing world communications, defusing hurricanes, allocating the fresh water of the planet.

Senator Claiborne Pell of Rhode Island, speaking at the

Newport Naval Base in 1967, called for an open space treaty
with all nations for a more orderly use of the sea. "We stand
on the threshold of a vast technical breakthrough, which may
suddenly advance our ability to carry out every type of
oceanologic activity, at any depth, and in any area of the
ocean." He pointed to the supranational treaty of Antarctica
as a model to follow.

A VISIT TO THE UNITED NATIONS

A visitor entering the great hall of the Security Council in
New York for the first time might well look about him in
astonishment. The amended Charter says that the Council is
to be a small body of 15 members, 5 permanent—the U.S.,
U.S.S.R., Britain, France, and China—with 10 members from
other countries, elected for two years only. But here is room
for hundreds of people. When an important issue is under discussion, the hall is sure to be well filled. One occasion in 1965
impressed me especially. The important issue that day concerned the war in Kashmir, where a UN cease-fire was tem-
porarily in force.

Clerks, reporters, visitors, members of the Assembly, walk
about under the great, staring wall mural. Arthur Goldberg,
the U.S. Ambassador, is on the move from chair to chair, his
white thatch conspicuous. Lord Caradon, the British Ambassador, rests an elbow on the table, hand on chin, and nods
laconically. U Thant, Secretary General, sits quietly beside the
President at the head of the table, apparently lost in meditation.

Here on one wing of the horseshoe table, a delegate occupies a chair marked "Pakistan"; on the other wing is an empty
chair marked "India." Neither nation is a member of the
Council, but both have been invited today to state their position in respect to the Council's cease-fire order in Kashmir.
Violations have been reported by both belligerents. The dis-

cussion proceeds with short speeches by members from the
U.S.S.R., the Ivory Coast, and Jordan. As we listen with our
earphones, the burden of the remarks clearly favors maintaining the cease-fire.

Inside the horseshoe table is a smaller square table with half
a dozen official secretaries. Outside, behind each member's
chair sit resource aides, who lean forward and whisper from
time to time. Back of them is a ring of open space, a railing,
and then chairs for members of the Assembly, all of them
filled today. The U.S. and the U.S.S.R. members, though not
in close agreement, seem to be running a parallel course in the
interest of stopping the war in Kashmir.

Back of the spacious press balcony is the huge gallery for
the public, every seat equipped with a hearing device which
offers us simultaneous translations in five languages. (When a
world language arrives, this device can be reduced to simple
amplification.) High up on either side of the mural are square
openings with TV cameras jutting out of them.

An empty chair for India, but the debate goes on. The war
over Kashmir has been halted, and down there are the 15 men
whose unanimous decision for cease-fire stopped it. Will it
remain stopped? If not, will it escalate? Down there men from
Africa, the Americas, the Near East, Russia, England, and
France may have the fate of the world in their hands.

CARETAKER GOVERNMENT

Four members of the Nuclear Club are sitting at the Council's table. The fifth member, Red China, is theoretically rep-
resented by the tiny segment of China on the Island of Formosa. This makes some historical sense, but no practical sense
at all in the Nuclear Age. The machinery for settling disputes
and for keeping the peace, which, in all logic, must *precede*
demilitarization, as Walter Millis made clear, requires cooperation by the entire Nuclear Club, including mainland China.

The club, indeed, may possibly become a kind of caretaker government during this critical period. The fundamental assumption of the UN Charter, that the five Great Powers should combine to keep the peace, retains its validity.

U Thant emphasized the point in an interview with Drew Middleton. He believes that unanimity of the big powers is cardinal in dealing with serious disputes between nations. There can be no lasting solution, he says, without this over-all agreement. Meanwhile UN power seems to be moving from the Assembly to the Council, a move, which, like coexistence, is probably unavoidable. It is difficult to see how the Assembly, 122 nations, with equal representation—where the vote of Barbados equals that of Russia or the United States—can hold the line in a time of volcanic change.

TWENTY YEARS

If the United Nations did not exist, it would have to be invented. Its roots are now so deep that only World War III could extinguish it. "The vital principle of the UN," Walter Lippmann once said, "is the enduring need for a meeting place where the governments can, whenever they choose to do so, talk privately about anything." How to end the Korean War, he observes, was outlined over martinis in the delegates' lounge. How to end the Berlin blockade was sketched out in the lobby.

The first considerable achievement of the UN was defending South Korea from being overrun from the north; Douglas MacArthur was technically a UN general in this operation. Then came crises in which the UN played a useful part: in Greece, Iran, Kashmir (1949), Berlin, Palestine, Suez, the Congo, Indonesia, Yemen, Laos, Cyprus, and Kashmir again in 1965. The limited Test Ban Treaty was negotiated in 1963 with UN approval, and military operations in outer space have been outlawed by resolution. The UN helped in the Cuba crisis. The great plans for a permanent international police force, however, have not been realized; nor have the hopes for a powerful, independent Secretariat. "Gradually," says Leonard Beaton in his excellent book, *The Struggle for Peace,* "the UN is getting some idea of what it can and cannot do. What the UN is, in essence, is the *agent* for the major powers . . . its function has been to find an area of common ground between the Big Powers."

Benjamin V. Cohen, one of UN's profound students, sees an international mind slowly developing in the Secretariat. By that he means the beginnings of a world culture, whose members give first loyalty to mankind. This is strange doctrine for a politician—though it would not be strange for a great religious leader. Mr. Cohen is dubious about the appointed members of both the Assembly and the Security Council. They have, he says, done very little in the last 20 years to develop the UN's machinery for peace-keeping. The member governments, while loudly proclaiming that there is no alternative to peace, give most of their attention to building up a military establishment.

The official UN delegates tend to think of themselves as stout defenders of their own nation's rights and perquisites, much as a Congressman from an American state may give higher priority to what he can secure for his home area than to what is best for America as a whole. On the other hand, Trygve Lie, Dag Hammerskjöld, and U Thant have held to the primacy of mankind; so have many in the Secretariat, and in many of the affiliated agencies, such as UNESCO and UNICEF. Indeed, members must take an oath to that effect, and their day-by-day duties reinforce it. Many more of us, in and out of the UN, should learn to follow this philosophy.

U Thant has given a clear account of what it means to be a world man, closely connected in his case with the Buddhist religion. He says:

I was brought up in a conservative Buddhist family and was trained to respect and observe the essentials of Buddhism. Among others, I was trained to achieve a certain degree of emotional equilibrium or detachment (which is one of the essential teachings of Lord Buddha). I was also trained to regard humanity as a whole and not in terms of segments or divisions. . . . I began to view things from a human point of view and not from a national point of view.

We must not forget that nuclear war has changed the characteristics of a true patriot. If, as Secretary McNamara has affirmed, an all-out thermonuclear exchange can eliminate both the U.S. and the U.S.S.R. as viable societies, then every loyal American, and every loyal Russian, must do his utmost to prevent a thermonuclear exchange, in order to save his country. If a citizen takes the traditional attitude of "my country right or wrong," pledged to fight for every scrap of national honor and every foot of sacred soil, the probability is high that he will lose his country. The fact that the enemy will also lose his country is scant consolation. This seems to be the logic of patriotism in the nuclear age. A national government armed with atomic weapons which uses those weapons to support preatomic policies is, as Hans Morgenthau has pointed out, in danger of becoming the enemy of its own people.

FINANCING THE UNITED NATIONS

Among other serious handicaps, the pitifully small and uncertain budget of the UN has plagued the organization from the start. The total, including affiliates, is less than one percent of what member nations spend for their armaments every year: one percent for peace, 99 percent for war. A modern state is obviously not a peace-loving enterprise. On the contrary: appropriations for war in the billions go roaring through the U.S. Senate, with only one or two Senators to register isolated votes against them; small appropriations for projects of peace may be buried in committee and never come to a vote.

With a lot more money the UN could take many more steps toward realizing one world. U Thant can readily suggest an agenda, beginning with adequate funds for peace-keeping and inspection by UN police forces. It has proved extremely difficult to extract more money from the various member states. Fortunately, however, another source of income is being opened up by technology, in an amount that staggers the imagination! Friends of the UN are asking why it should not share in the riches which will soon be available, and belong to no individual and to no nation, but to all mankind?

As noted in Chapter 7, minerals as yet unreclaimed in sea water will be extracted by electrolysis, using cheap nuclear energy. Manganese, cobalt, copper, and nickel may be mined on the ocean floor by new techniques. There are 60 million tons of phosphate off the California coast beyond national limits, and titanium sands off Florida, India, Japan, and Australia, beyond national claim. There is unknown wealth to be dredged by Operation Mohole from deep sea bottoms, and still more by mining the earth's mantle, using remote controls. Why not give the UN royalty rights on all these minerals?

It has been suggested that the UN share financially in certain new synthetic foods processed from the algae of the oceans. Why should it not share in the growing income from communication satellites like Telstar? Why not a percentage of the tolls from the projected sea-level canal to be cut across the Isthmus of Panama? Or royalties on various new products to be derived from atomic research in medicine?

There are possibilities in many directions, all tied to the growth of technology. Give the UN title to wealth which as yet belongs to nobody—and incidentally thereby prevent wholesale piracy and bitter national disputes.[1]

[1] Clark N. Eichelberger of the UN can furnish a formidable list.

ANTARCTICA AS A PORTENT

The seventh continent contains fabulous resources which technology can gradually make available. The UN might well share in their exploitation. Antarctica is already a supranational agency. The treaty to which both the U.S. and the U.S.S.R. adhere was signed by the 12 nations with interests in the Antarctic, at Canberra, Australia, in 1961. It provides that the continent shall be used only for peaceful purposes and shall contain no military bases. It suspends all territorial claims to the Antarctic, and stipulates that all activities in the region be open to inspection by observers designated by the nations signing the treaty. Scientific information gathered by anyone must be made available to all, and personnel are to be exchanged among the several stations. Soviet scientists are now working in American stations, and vice versa.[2] Antarctica is a landmark in the trend toward one world.

A FIVE-POINT FOREIGN POLICY

Well, what is the net effect of these variables, plus and minus, on the trend to peace? How great is the Great Hope? I believe we can give it high probability under five conditions:

1. If Russia and the United States can maintain a strong *détente*.

2. If the proliferation of nuclear weapons can be contained. The Nuclear Club will have to unite on this.

3. If deterrence can hold until the machinery for settling disputes between nations is firmly in place, with legislature, courts, and police power. The UN Charter will have to be revised so that the body can act as well as talk, and also forego the disrupting veto in the Security Council. This may call for a

---

[2] *New York Times,* November 30, 1965. The *Times* hopes that a similar agreement can be worked out for the moon, "a solar body to be ruled by the U.N."

new chamber empowered to pass mandatory legislation[3]

4. If accidental nuclear explosions can be prevented from escalating, by means of safety devices such as "hot lines," and restraint on the part of chiefs of state.

5. And if mainland China in due time becomes a responsible member of the Nuclear Club, and of the United Nations.

The *détente* between the two great superpowers is cardinal in the dangerous years immediately ahead. Said Drew Middleton in September, 1967: "The only time the United Nations operates with any success in keeping the peace is when the interests of the United States and the Soviet Union coincide. That was true over Kashmir in 1965, and it has been true this year over the Middle East to the extent that both superpowers wanted the fighting stopped." How can the United Nations be effective, Middleton asks, as long as the U.S. and the U.S.S.R. are at odds?

Here is, I believe, a guideline for the foreign policy of any nation, particularly for the five nuclear powers. Perhaps these conditions are too difficult. Perhaps cultural lag will not permit their exercise for years to come. Who knows? But the alternative is blunt. As long as there is a margin of probability, men and women of good will are in duty bound to act upon it.

[3] As outlined by the Peace-Keeping Ways and Means Committee in New York.

14

IN SEARCH OF A RESULTANT

IN PHYSICS, according to Webster, a resultant is "a force with an effect equal to that of two or more forces acting together." Thus if we had a body being pulled in a number of directions like this:

the body would move in only one direction, which would be the resultant of these forces, say like this:

In a study of trends which influence one another more or less heavily, and which are not often subject to exact measurement, we cannot plot a mathematical resultant. We can, however, make a rough estimate of the combined effect on the body at issue, in this case human welfare, which is a rather high abstraction. Will the effect be positive, negative, or neutral? What we want is an answer to a fairly simple question: Will our children's children have a better life?

Allen Upward, in his book *The New Word,*[1] remarked that he could not be bothered to pay his bills, as he spent so much of his time in the twenty-first century. Well, we have been spending some time there, what with one exponential curve and another, though even more time in the late years of the twentieth century. What useful reports can we bring back?

Any careful assessment of gains and losses due to technology makes it perfectly clear that we now confront an era more hazardous than any previous one in human history. In order to take advantage of the gains—such as unlimited energy from the atom—and to deal with the losses—such as a runaway population rate—the leaders of mankind, if not the mass, will have to develop some new intellectual tools. They must depend on the social sciences, for example, to help design political and economic machinery for a world without war. Let us briefly summarize the ten trends with which we have been concerned.

THE TEN TRENDS

1. *Total technology*

Pure science opened the door to applied science, and today is partly combined with it in the concept of R & D. Both have been growing at an exponential rate ever since Galileo firmly anchored the scientific method more than three centuries ago. Pure science alone—say, quantum theory—has little effect on the human condition beyond academic discourse. Usually, however, pure science is put to work in a new machine, a new technique, a new weapon. Who could have predicted the profound effect on the human condition of $E = mc^2$?

These steeply rising curves have driven some philosophers,

[1] Mitchell Kennerly, 1910.

like Jacques Ellul, and some scientists, like Max Born, to repudiate not only Western technology, but science itself. If exponential growth continues on all fronts up to the year 2000, the pessimists would undoubtedly be vindicated. The planet is only so big, with strict limits on its supplies of air, fresh water, and living space. Fortunately, as Professor John R. Platt has emphasized, some of these growth curves are going to falter and bend backward into S-curves.

2. *Population*

Living space contracts as population expands, while the man-land ratio worsens. Technology has generated two great expansions since Galileo. The first came with the industrial revolution, the second with modern medicine and its reduction of the death rate. At present rates of growth, the world's population will double by the end of the century.

Growth rates are uneven—low in Western Europe and Japan, medium in the United States and Russia, high in Latin America, Africa, and most of Asia, where hunger, poverty, and illiteracy are increasing. At present growth rates, it can be only a matter of time before affluent societies, too, outrun their resources.

For the immediate crisis more food can be grown, but, as Malthus demonstrated long ago, there can be no stability when a population grows faster than its nutrients. Stability for the long run can be achieved in two ways: by birth control or by an equilibrium established by famine. Japan has demonstrated the feasibility of the first method. Has the rest of the world time enough to follow Japan's example?

3. *Living space*

Only about one-eighth of the earth's surface is fit for human habitation. This modest percentage is now under attack from the pollution of the air, particularly due to car exhausts; from pollution of rivers, lakes, and coastal waters; from decline in fresh-water supplies; from pollution and destruction of the soil by erosion, refuse dumps, pesticides, open-pit mining; from the proliferation of noise, with sonic boom on the trend curve; from nuclear fallout, with its long-term genetic effects; from the disruption of the Van Allen belt in outer space, which protects us from excessive radiation; from attempts to control the weather, including the "greenhouse effect," in which carbon dioxide raises the earth's average temperature. A growing conservation movement is trying to cope with these attacks.

4. *Megalopolis*

Technology has encouraged a world-wide migration from farms to cities. In affluent societies an outward migration to the suburbs is also massive. A city-suburban complex is now called the "urban field" and is beset with problems. New York City, for example, is suffering from traffic jams, power failures, water shortages, smog, crippling strikes, crime waves, race riots, school crises, and financial stringency, while its suburbs are filled with superhighways, supermarkets, filling stations, roadhouses, factories, gravel pits, and garbage dumps. A few "new towns" such as Reston, Virginia, are being built, and there is some talk of mass transport to replace commuting by private car, talk of pedestrian malls, of electric automobiles which create no lethal fumes.

5. *Energy*

The whole technological complex is largely based on cheap, abundant energy from coal, oil, and gas. These fuels will not last indefinitely, but atomic power via the fission of uranium is moving in. By A.D. 2000 it may be the major source of energy, limited by the supply of uranium. If scientists can devise a workable method for atomic fusion, the hydrogen of the oceans can be used as raw material—100 quadrillion tons of it—and the energy problem solved.

Cheap atomic power can provide fresh water by desalting sea water in vast quantities, permit the exploitation of shales and minerals now too costly to extract, and even produce synthetic materials at reasonable cost.

6. *The mixed economy*

This is another strong trend on the asset side. The growing mix of public and private activity tends to dissolve the rigid ideologies of both capitalism and Communism. In combination with abundant atomic power, and with birth control, it may go far to solve the world's economic problems.

7. *Automation*

Labor-saving devices, led by the computer, are encouraging more production and more unemployment. Automation may thus be classified as both asset and liability. It can eliminate a great deal of dull, monotonous labor, but if unrelieved idleness is the end result, the cure may be worse than the disease. The evidence strongly indicates that man is a working animal —in the sense of needing an activity that involves hand and brain, and that makes sense to him.

8. *The arms race*

This trend is still rapidly rising. A drive for antimissile missiles is building up in both the U.S. and the U.S.S.R. The old habits, and old war cries persist. If nuclear proliferation cannot be stopped, the deterrence shield will certainly be breached. The five members of the Nuclear Club, not all on speaking terms, are now confronted with the supreme irony of war in the atomic age: *the more powerful their weapons, the less their security.* Chiefs of state sometimes admit this verbally, but they act on it only with the greatest reluctance. The facts of technology seem to be 30 years ahead of their thinking and acting.

9. *Nationalism*

This trend goes in two contrary directions. The dismantling of the British, French, Belgian, and Dutch empires has created scores of new nations, and so enormously extended the institution of nationalism. At the same time technology is forcing new forms of internationalism and supranationalism—some 2,000 agencies are reported in Chapter 13. The European Common Market is an outstanding example.

As population outruns food supply, the future of the new nations as independent states is very dubious. Regional associations appear to be mandatory.

10. *One world*

Although there can be no enduring peace without disarmament, it is equally logical that general disarmament first demands some strong supranational authority to settle disputes between nations, and enforce decisions. The United Nations is laying the groundwork, but is not yet trusted by the Great Powers.

The next immediate step would seem to be a firm agreement between the United States and Russia to halt the spread of nuclear weapons. Beyond that would come action to the same end by all members of the Nuclear Club.

The technological imperative is overriding national frontiers by air, sea, land, stratosphere, and outer space. Technology is shaping the outlines of one world, whatever the politicians may choose to do about it.

ESTIMATING THE RESULTANT

The above summary shows six rapidly ascending curves: population, Megalopolis, energy, armaments, automation, and technology as a whole. It shows one rapidly descending curve: living space on the planet, with the resources necessary to life and well-being. It shows three qualitative trends which cannot be measured in any statistical form: the mixed economy, nationalism, and, per contra, the trend to one world. Again we must remind ourselves that this is an arbitrary selection, and other trends (of less importance, as it seems to me) are also at work, to complicate the conditions of life to which our children must try to adjust themselves.

The six ascending curves seem to be increasing exponentially, like compound interest, and so is the negative curve of living space—its losses are exponential. Now exponential growth, if continued indefinitely, will rise right off the top of the map, to become an explosion!

Will any or all of these trends reach the point of sudden explosion, to destroy everything around? The arms race might do just that, but the others will require more time—even the population explosion is a slowly developing phenomenon. The trends influence each other, and through them the resultant. Thus the dangerous rate of population stands in opposition to the life-destroying potential of a nuclear exchange, so that, as Joseph Wood Krutch once suggested half-seriously, many problems could be solved by a war that was "just large enough." Again, the mixed economy as it expands could cause the arms race to slacken by reducing ideological tensions between "capitalists" and "Communists." These are only a few of the many possible interactions.

Now let us try a rough evaluation, as follows:

Trend	Predominantly Asset	Predominantly Liability	Strongly Both
1. Total technology			✔
2. Population growth		✔	
3. Shrinkage of living space...........		✔	
4. Megalopolis		✔	
5. Peaceful energy from the atom......	✔		
6. The mixed economy	✔		
7. Automation			✔
8. The arms race		✔	
9. Nationalism			✔
10. One world	✔		

Our judgment of this table must be more or less subjective, both as to impact and as to timing. There is little difficulty, however, in coming to a firm conclusion if the trends are pushed to their exponential limits. The automation curve leads finally to machines doing all the work and men doing nothing at all, with consequent biological damage; one world leads to universal brotherhood and the dream of Tennyson; population growth leads to standing room only.

The accounting, for what it is worth, suggests that we need not quite despair. It suggests that Messrs. Ellul and Born have thrown up their hands too soon in predicting what technology promises for the human condition. It indicates—at least to me—that the race is close,with a small probability in favor of the positive, though even the canniest computer could not assess all the variables and give us a mathematical resultant.

What does emerge very clearly is the necessity of taking all the trends into consideration before soaring off on one of them as conclusive for the whole complex. Such a finding may be permissible for No. 8, the arms race, if the certified end of the race is World War III. That end, however, has not been certified; other trends, especially No. 10, intervene. The great hope runs parallel to the great peril.

We can be reasonably sure that the years will be rough up to the end of the century; sure that affluent citizens dedicated to having total fun and total comfort will be most uncomfortably disappointed. Even the chromium-plated loved one, trailing nitrous oxides, may be denied them. After the turbulence—that shock front, in Dr. Platt's vivid analogy—the world might emerge into an era of relative stability, as S-curves hold down some of the more ominous exponentials.

The three major liabilities are (1) population, (2) living space, and (3) the arms race—"Babies, Bulldozers, and Bombs," as I once phrased it, but in a different order. These three, in whatever order you please to place them, claim priority for analysis and constructive action. Every chief of state should put them at the top of his agenda; no thinking citizen should lose sight of their primary importance.

OF HUMAN KNOWLEDGE

The final resultant, I believe, depends more on human knowledge, and its application by human beings, than it does on the curves of technology. It goes back in the end to people.

What human countertrends are discernible, and how can they
be implemented? Will there be enough mature citizens around
to steer the twentieth century through the coming shock front
and into the calm beyond? The condition of man will be con-
ditioned eventually by the behavior of men.

By way of encouragement we may now introduce two more
well-documented trends:

First, the sharp increase in college enrollments in America,
and in the West generally, is enlarging the talent pool
from which future leaders will mostly be drawn.

Second, the steady development of the behavioral sciences
offers the most effective kind of applied science with
which to understand and to deal with the impact of
technology.

Let us briefly consider each:

EDUCATION AND TOLERANCE

As affluent societies send more and more young people to
college, the level of literacy rises—not always in direct proportion to numbers, for many students seem allergic to academic infusions. But literacy still goes up; students are at least
exposed to ideas, to research and objective inquiry. The fasci-
nation of the comics begins to fade, and the new attitudes are
measurable.

A poll of adult Americans conducted by Elmo Roper in
1960 posed the question: "Was the Supreme Court's decision
for racial integration in public schools a mistake?" Respondents in the sample were classified by their education, with
these highly significant results:

	It was a mistake
Citizen with grade school education only	40 percent
Some high school	24 percent
Some college	20 percent
College graduates	15 percent

Thus almost three times as many grade-schoolers as college graduates disapproved of the Supreme Court's decision outlawing the segregation of Negroes in public schools. In other public opinion surveys, most American college students say that they go to college to have fun, or to prepare themselves for getting a well-paid job. Whatever their announced goals, however, the solid fact remains that the more years boys and girls spend in school, the more tolerant and liberal, on the average, they become.

The late Dr. Samuel Stouffer, sociologist at Harvard, in a survey of attitudes toward civil liberties in the U.S., worked out a "scale of tolerance" based on education. On this scale, college graduates rated a tolerance of 66 percent, high school graduates 42 percent, grade schoolers 16 percent. "People knowing little," Stouffer concluded, "are ill-equipped to adjust to a world in motion."

Again, surveys show that the higher the respondent's education, the more likely he is to regard the United Nations as vital to world peace, and to hope that it will be made stronger. At the same time, the better-educated respondents say they are not satisfied with the current performance of the UN. Far from wanting to abolish it, however, as do many of the less educated, they want to improve it.

Now if college students hold these attitudes on large social issues, whatever their personal goals, it follows that the greater the number of educated people in a given community, the better the prospect for dealing wisely with the population crisis, the arms race, and the bulldozer. Young people, furthermore, can detect and resist cultural lag better than their parents. Paul Goodman has made this point:

Half our population is under 25. Forty percent of the college-age group is in college, six million at present, and these students, the dominant inheritors of our society, are the best hope, finally the sole hope, of altering our doombound course.[2]

[2] *New Republic*, January 7, 1967.

Clark Kerr, ex-president of the University of California, whose experience with the college-age group is probably unexcelled, describes three main student types: the political activists, running energetically around with placards; the Bohemians, growing beards and shedding shoes; and the new collegiates, not so keen about football and increasingly aware of the world they live in—"born under the sign of the bomb." The last group is by far the most numerous, though the sign carriers and the hippies get all the publicity. Its members do not parade much, but they have read *1984* and *Brave New World;* they know about IBM cards and are shy of a computerized world.

Nobody pays much attention to them, but in my opinion they are setting the tone of this generation. The campus revolutionaries are never going to win; this is not a revolutionary country. And the alienated Bohemians are parasites. What is most significant about this generation is the very high proportion of the Peace Corps type.[3]

THE BEHAVIORAL SCIENCES

A second encouraging trend is the steady development of the social sciences— particularly cultural anthropology, social psychology, and sociology, disciplines which deal primarily with human behavior. In my book, *The Proper Study of Mankind,* I tried to indicate what the social sciences have already accomplished, to what they aspire, together with a list of "great unanswered questions." Berelson and Steiner, in a massive inventory some years later, have gone on to list more than one thousand verified conclusions in the study of human bebehavior.[4] These findings, say the authors, "refer to important statements of proper generality for which there is some good amount of scientific evidence." How do the findings go? They

[3] *New York Times* magazine, June 4, 1967.
[4] B. Berelson and G. A. Steiner, *Human Behavior,* Harcourt, Brace & World, 1964.

are carefully numbered, with first a statement, and then some factual support:

A1. Human behavior is far more variable, and therefore less predictable, than that of any other species. . . .

A1.1 Human behavior is more dependent upon learning and less regulated by instinct than the behavior of lower animals. . . .

A2. Man achieves maximum flexibility in behavior, but the process requires prolonged childhood dependence—by far the longest in the animal world, as measured in portion of life span. In contrast to an insect, man not only can, but must, learn his fundamental repertoire of adaptive behavior if he is to survive.

The authors comment on the above: "From this one fact alone stem many far-reaching behavioral implications—from the universality of the family, to the personality characteristics that derive from his period of dependency."

This is about as far as the authors go by way of comment. Such statements may seem obvious, especially by contrast with sensational popular theories about the nature of monkeys and porpoises as applied to men. Obvious as they are, they are widely ignored and even contradicted. Yet can we deal effectively with our human predicaments, both social and personal, unless knowledge of this kind is compiled, verified, and put to work?

THE FAMILY

Let us return, for instance, to proposition *A2*, the universality of the family. This is a fact of transcendent importance. The institution of the family is clearly being hurt by the pressures and tensions of Megalopolis, especially by the unprecedented mobility afforded by the motorcar, with millions of families on the move. But if *A2* is scientifically sound, as I believe it to be, such disruption of the family must have a limit. A stable environment, whether tribal, peasant-agricultural, or technological, *must* be firmly in place—not for moral reasons, if you please, but simply to shelter, care for, and bring to maturity the young of the species. It takes up to 18 years of family stability to accomplish this, in any culture, at any time. Without it we get Harlem, and Joseph Lyford's dreadful account of children who have ceased to be human. Trends which are weakening the institution of the family not only ought to be reversed by deliberate planning, but ultimately *will* be reversed by blind nature, though she may have to take us back to the Stone Age in the process. The family, normally monogamous, is the one universal human institution that cannot be tampered with indefinitely.

One could cite hundreds of accredited findings from the inventory found in *Human Behavior,* findings which are applicable to current problems. We have here an accessible storehouse of dependable knowledge. There are many empty shelves, to be sure, many questions unanswered; but year by year the knowledge grows, ready to hand for decision-makers. To expect the science of behavior to expand at a rate comparable to that of solid-state physics is of course wildly Utopian; but considering its importance today, it deserves more encouragement than physics, and far more than it is getting. Even one percent of the money now lavished on the arms race—say, a billion dollars a year for research in human behavior—would be enormously useful. Take, for instance, two urgent necessities: better psychological methods for making people aware of the danger of the arms race; and again, improved techniques for expanding birth control throughout the various cultures of the underdeveloped world. Both are challenges to the social sciences, rather than to the natural sciences.

The impact of technology is warping and stretching, when not actively disintegrating, many of our fundamental institutions. The family is under heavy pressure as we have noted.

Megalopolis is far off balance. Political parties are losing their traditional outlines. Private property and its established rules cannot cope with outer space, the earth's mantle, air and water pollution, supranationalism.

An enormous task faces the social sciences in helping us adjust to these changes.

THE ABILITY TO THINK

In close alignment with trends in college enrollments and in the behavioral sciences is an interesting experiment being conducted in Berkeley, California. It tends to verify a conclusion often emphasized by biologists such as Julian Huxley: *The normal human brain is almost never used at capacity.* It can handle more input than it is ever likely to be charged with.

Dr. Richard S. Crutchfield, with help from the Carnegie Corporation, has been working with children in the Berkeley public schools in an attempt to bring out some of that potential.[5] In an early experiment he took children in the fifth and sixth grades and gave them a six-hour pre-test. As a result, 481 of them were selected as roughly equal in ability. He then divided these into two groups, A and B. To the 267 children in Group A he gave a series of exercises in problem-solving which had been carefully worked out in advance. They revolved around simple detective stories which held the children's interest. What had happened? How could the guilty person be found? Group B, with 214 children, became the scientific control in the experiment, and continued with normal class work.

At the end of a given period, children in both groups were given an eight-hour post-test to measure changes in their ability to think and reason, compared with the pre-test. "The findings," said Crutchfield, "are clear. The trained children in

[5] Published by Educational Testing Service, Princeton, New Jersey, 1965.

Group A showed a marked superiority in performance over the control children in Group B." This was true of every test problem without exception. The trained children were able to generate about twice as many acceptable ideas for solving a given problem as the children in the control group. Children with relatively low IQ's in Group A, after training, surpassed children with relatively high IQ's in Group B.

More research is needed, but obviously here in Berkeley is strong evidence of mental capacity normally unused, and a way to develop it. Says Dr. Crutchfield in summing up:

We have been guided by the belief that virtually every child—regardless of his level of intelligence, school achievement, or socio-economic background—can substantially benefit from explicit training in creative thinking. . . . There is an enormous gap between his usual performance and the performance he is really capable of.

The program gets away from the "one correct answer" idea which is implicit in so much of our traditional schooling, to find many different answers. "Our aim is to reinforce this diversity."

These youngsters will be in their forties when the twentieth century ends. The world could well use a few million from Group A.

BACK TO THE RESULTANT

The rough table of assets and liabilities posed on page 199 indicated, from the author's point of view at least, a close race. The technological trends which are aiding, or can be expected to aid, the human condition over the next three decades will, it seems to him, win out against the negative trends. Meanwhile the more youngsters who can stay in school, and the better they learn to use their minds, the sounder the decisions which will be made, and the more hopeful the chance for a positive resultant.

If deterrence will hold, if the United Nations can be strengthened, with China firmly incorporated, and if legislative machinery can be set up for handling disputes between nations, we can weather the shock front. But whatever calm we may find beyond will still be seriously agitated by failure to control population. The over-all growth rate will, I think, be down, but not far enough down to avoid famine in some areas of the Hungry World, accompanied by acute political upheavals.

What conclusion does the reader draw? Given these ten trends, together with possibilities for expanding and improving education—for which there is already some evidence—does he also see rather more than a glimmer of hope? In the famous race between education and catastrophe will the reader, on the evidence, back education?

There is no possibility of escaping the trends. There they are in plain sight, for anyone not blinded by ideology.

In coming to his own estimate of a resultant, the reader should never forget, even in his blackest moments, that technology has made large wars obsolete; and if population can be controlled by medical and social science, technology will make poverty obsolete.

☆

15

NO PATH BUT KNOWLEDGE

THIS STUDY has stayed fairly close to well-documented trends. A number of uptrends in opposition to downtrends have been mentioned—such as electric- instead of gasoline-powered motorcars—but little in the way of an all-round constructive program.

I doubt if such a single program can be found, but in this final chapter two wide-ranging suggestions, hopefully constructive, will be offered. The first is a proposed curriculum for the training of future political leaders. The second is a call for a supranational agency—a kind of bureau of standards—to evaluate and screen the consequences of large technological innovations, *before* they go into mass production, seriously to affect the culture.

It was H. G. Wells, I believe, who once said: "There is no path but knowledge out of the jungles of life." If we are in a jungle today—as this study amply demonstrates—where is the knowledge to lead us out? And who can do the leading? The current political leadership—with perhaps the lonely exception of U Thant—seems to be badly entangled in the underbrush, unable to adjust old political habits to new technological realities.

What are the prospects for developing leaders better aware of these realities from the youngsters now in school? One of them said to me not long ago: "I know we're in trouble and I'd like to help. What should I study?" Well, what should he study? What should young potential leaders all over the world study? Clark Kerr believes there are a lot of them.

FORTY PERCENT

We have noted how 40 percent of all young people of college age in the United States are now in college, and how that gross statistical fact is making for more open-mindedness and tolerance, regardless of many grave drawbacks in those colleges, regardless of any announced goals by students for better jobs or just having a good time. We have also noted that the human mind is seldom used at capacity, and cited Dr. Crutchfield's method, as tested in the public schools of Berkeley, for developing more of its potential. Thus there seems to be some margin in which to maneuver as technology moves in on us.

It has been estimated that in the next 20 years Americans between 35 and 65 years of age will increase by less than 11 million, those between 20 and 34 by 25 million, while those *under 20 will increase by 35 million!*[1] "The center of our political stage," the report giving these statistics continues, "is now being taken over by a new power group—a professional, technical and managerial class, very young, affluent, and highly educated. It will soon replace the old power centers— labor, the farm bloc, and Big Business." Another significant statistic is that a full half of the U.S. population today is under 25 years old.

School and college enrollments are increasing. Students are given better texts and teaching materials, while the computer is being used to improve individual performance, by helping students advance at their own pace. But a far more radical policy is in prospect. The National Education Association and the American Association of School Administrators are pro-

[1] U.S. Senate Republican Policy Committee, 1966.

posing that education be oriented around the "spirit of science."[2] They define this spirit by seven attributes:

1. A desire to know
2. An impulse to question
3. The search for data
4. The demand for verification
5. Respect for logic
6. Awareness of premises
7. Evaluation of consequences

This forthright if not revolutionary proposal does not recommend that students be educated as scientists, or that they study intensively the subject matter of any branch of science. *It recommends a method of thinking.* "The values of which the spirit of science consists should permeate the educative process, serving as objectives of learning in every field, including the humanities."

It is news indeed when powerful policy-makers propose such a change. Education, they insist, should now be reoriented to close the gap between the sciences and the humanities, the gap made famous by C. P. Snow. Every student should become familiar with the scientific attitude, even though his life's work may be devoted to an analysis of the Upanishads.

The spirit and values of science can enable each person to free himself from blind obedience to the dictates of his emotions, of propaganda, of group pressures, of the authority of others. . . . It can enable him to sift through the forces which act upon him. . . . It can enable entire peoples to use their minds with breadth and dignity. . . . It promotes individuality. It can strengthen man's efforts in behalf of world community.[3]

With this call to action from the very heartland of the American educational establishment—the NEA and the

[2] Editorial in *Science,* June 24, 1966.
[3] *Current,* November, 1966.

School Administrators—we need not be unduly hesitant in proposing a curriculum for future leaders, who are in school today.

NOTES FOR A CURRICULUM

Father Henle, vice president of St. Louis University, sets the stage. "We do not have anywhere in the United States," he says, "a college curriculum which is truly modern and which at the same time does for the modern student what a 'liberal' education was expected to do for the student in the Renaissance, or in the nineteenth century." The nonscience majors today, Father Henle continues, are both illiterate and ignorant. But the science majors are also ignorant. Ignorant of what? Ignorant of the kind of world we live in, ignorant of how to make decisions in the nuclear age.

Our candidate for leadership must be a *generalist,* as well as a specialist in some particular field. He—or she—must constantly be asking: "How does *this* relate to *that?*" How does automation relate to leisure, and how does leisure relate to human nature? How does cheap nuclear energy relate to the hunger of the Hungry World?

A generalist tries to get all the major characteristics in before coming to a conclusion. For instance, he does not instantly condemn the white people of Mississippi for their racial intolerance. Rather, a generalist asks: "How were they brought up? What are the belief systems of the local culture?" If he himself had been reared in a typical white family of the Deep South, he knows the probability is high that he would react to the historic decision of the Supreme Court much as they do. He knows that prejudice is not subject to legislation, but where one sits in a bus can be legislated, and ultimately will modify prejudice.

It is cardinal that our candidate be not handicapped by a rigid ideology. The current systems of belief in a culture must be noted as given—fully understood if not fully accepted, as in the matter of race prejudice. But any imposed political or economic cult will destroy a candidate's usefulness. The jungle is crawling with cults, blindly followed, from the Ku Klux Klan to the Black Muslims.

One danger of ideology is that it prevents further learning. If one's ideology explains everything, why bother to learn more? I remember a cartoon showing an editor of a Marxist paper in New York waving an Associated Press dispatch at an assistant. "Class angle that, Joe," the caption read.

A study of cultural anthropology is perhaps the best solvent for rigid ideologies and dogmas. I would place it first on the curriculum. Following it might come:

> Communication theory
> An outline of biology
> An outline of human history since Sumeria
> A history of science and technology since Galileo
> Social psychology
> The new economics
> Aspects of international law

These are eight fundamental studies for the curriculum, all oriented around the scientific attitude, as recommended by the National Education Association. Let us briefly consider each.

CULTURAL ANTHROPOLOGY

Our candidate should begin it early as protection against creeping ideology, and at some point do a stint of field work. He will not have to go to New Guinea; he can do it in a neighboring town, as Warner and the Lynds did.[4] Anthropology is a cardinal tool for understanding people of all races, all cultures, all times. Ishi, the last Stone Age man in America, was thrown into jail by the California police, to be rescued by a renowned anthropologist. Together they offered the world a

---

[4] Newburyport, Massachusetts, and Muncie, Indiana.

superb example of the way all men are united by nature and divided by nurture.

It is impossible to escape from the culture that locks us in—locks every human being who ever lived. But a generalist can look over the walls, as Ruth Benedict said, and in doing so become more free than the most active reformer whose efforts are focused on an immediate breaking down of walls. Walls do not come down that way. Ishi and Dr. Kroeber had a gate through which they passed, back and forth, from the culture of A.D. 1000 to that of 1910.

Cultural anthropology is, I firmly believe, one of the two most important tools for future leadership, yet it is hard to think of a political leader in the world today who has any grasp of it. Margaret Mead has made a strong plea for its use.[5] Cultural evolution, she says, evolves through people; it is not something beyond human control; determined individuals can gradually change a culture. She gives an interesting example of how the Manus people of the Admiralty Islands in the Pacific shifted, without too much tension, from tribalism to the modern world under the determined leadership of one man, named Paliao. Cultural lag is always a drag on change, but it can be moved. There are plenty of highly gifted individuals around, but they have seldom been organized in a massed drive to change a culture. We need, says Margaret Mead, a conscious determination to outmaneuver cultural lag, based on usable knowledge about human behavior.

COMMUNICATION THEORY

The other primary tool for our candidate is an understanding of how words behave. He is helpless if entangled in the double-talk of commercial advertising, image-making, publicity appeals, economic forecasting, stock market analysis, traditional diplomacy, foreign policy pronouncements, selling

[5] *Continuities in Cultural Evolution,* Yale University Press, 1964.

the package rather than what is in it, most propaganda and campaign oratory. Adlai Stevenson succeeded in rising above the last when he insisted, in the 1956 Presidential campaign, on "talking sense." (Was Stevenson a prototype of leaders to come: too intelligent and too honest for his day?)

Communication theory can teach a leader how to be quiet and listen, how language can corrupt understanding as well as further it, how agreement and coexistence can be advanced. It can show him constructive ways to use the mass media, Telstar, the computer, the press conference, the official statement. On my desk is a motto on cedar wood given me by the late Beardsley Ruml: "Reasonable men always agree if they understand what they are talking about." With a slight question mark at the word "always," our candidate might well keep that motto handy for many occasions.

BIOLOGY

If he must choose one laboratory science, biology is probably the best. It gives him a never-to-be-forgotten insight into the delicate structure of an organism, however small, and its intricate physiological balance. Well taught, biology helps the student appreciate the values of ecology—the economy of nature and the hazards of disrupting it. Biology can show how slowly man evolved through millions of years by natural selection, and the impossibility of speeding this massive and time-consuming process. It will make him wary of brash predictions about controlling human heredity, and brash conclusions about communicating with intelligent beings on distant planets, and still warier of half-baked generalizations about human beings from the behavior of apes, fishes, and birds.

What we can do is to change our nurture, not our inherited nature, as emphasized by Margaret Mead. Since every child must learn it afresh, a decisive policy change in primary education could transform our current culture pretty rapidly, even its belligerent nationalism. A fundamental cultural change in nationalism is even now underway, as noted in Chapter 13, but can it change fast enough to control the nuclear threat?

HISTORY

Our candidate should be familiar with a running account of written history, beginning with the first cities in Sumeria, a span of 5,000 years. H. G. Wells's *Outline,* revised and brought up to date, would help to give him the necessary background. What has history to teach us, now that we have invented ourselves into the nuclear age?

Professor Elting Morison of the Massachusetts Institute of Technology, after impressive evidence that historical parallels are obsolete at the present rate of technological change, goes on to suggest various valuable insights that history *can* teach. It is still the best field, he says, in which to analyze the influence of the nonlogical elements that help to shape human life. It is the most likely place to look for all the elements that enter human situations—machines, ideas, money, geology, climate, hunger, fear, high hope. History seems to Morison the prime civilizing agency in the educational process. It can still create the sense of a past, without which "there can be no adequate awareness of the present, no real feeling for a possible future."

After such a study, the student would see why historical analogies must be made with great caution, especially after an enormous turning point such as that of Hiroshima. The ill-fated conference at Munich in 1938, for instance, between Hitler and Neville Chamberlain, is repeatedly cited today as an historical lesson in the folly of appeasement—better to stand up and fight! But there was no stock of overkill in 1938, no ICBM's, no Polaris submarines, and so no parallel whatever with a rational conduct of foreign policy in 1967. To stand up and fight a thermonuclear war today is to lose one's country.

HISTORY OF SCIENCE AND TECHNOLOGY

A candidate for leadership should also have a good working knowledge of the technical arts, beginning with Galileo. This carries out the recommendation of the National Education Association referred to above. He does not need condensed courses in physics or physiology so much as a thorough introduction to the scientific method. If our major problems spring from a developing technology, as this book insists, whoever hopes to deal with them must understand the process. He must learn to use his mind like a scientist. He must be aware of the three steps in human knowledge cited earlier: from folk knowledge, to written records, and on to science—where the record is often in the language of mathematics, and where the test is independent verification. In the first two chapters I tried to develop this idea.

SOCIAL PSYCHOLOGY

Our candidate must have a firm grasp on this discipline. The theory of frustration-aggression is almost completely neglected by our leaders in current foreign policy.[6] The daily headlines carry charges and countercharges of "aggression," as in the Israeli-Arab War; but a special committee of the UN, after some years of study, is still unable to define "aggression" in international relations. In current use, an "aggressor" is apparently any nation you do not like. Social psychology can supply useful knowledge about techniques of agreement— what kind of disputes can be negotiated and what cannot. It can throw light on the concept of coexistence, on the widespread habit of "denial" in facing threatening issues, on the limits of human comprehension, on crowd psychology; it can help in drafting the machinery for world government. Public opinion research, based on scientific sampling theory, is a de-

[6] John Dollard, Leonard W. Doob, and others, *Frustration and Aggression,* Yale University Press, 1939.

partment of social psychology, and of increasing value to intelligent leadership. It has little useful value in picking political winners, but great value in indicating how people in the mass feel about political issues.

THE NEW ECONOMICS

A course in Keynesian economics and the next step beyond, which we are now entering, will show our candidate how the mixed economy is invading every society, East and West, where high-energy conditions prevail. The new economics is dissolving rigid concepts of both "capitalism" and "Communism." Russia is expanding the area of private initiative for local management, while the United States is expanding the public sector, as noted earlier.

A good grounding in statistics is essential for an understanding of the new economics. How is the GNP arrived at? What is the basis for calculating the rate of unemployment? When should the levers be pulled to halt inflation or recession? How do banks create money, and how is the total money supply limited?

A future leader, as he studies the new economics, will find a stunning example of the dangers in two-valued thinking—that everything must be black or white with no middle ground; that the world must be either "capitalist" or "Communist." The John Birch Society and Red China are the foremost champions of such logic. The hard facts, however, are swarming into the middle ground. There are now about a dozen varieties of "Communism." The two chief varieties, centering in Peking and Moscow, are, as I write, near to armed clashes on their common Asiatic border.

ASPECTS OF INTERNATIONAL LAW

Far short of law school, a candidate should be familiar with the exciting prospects in *international and supranational law*.

Who, for instance, has property rights in the moon? (An up-and-coming realtor advertised lunar lots for sale—at $100 each, as I remember it.) What shall be the traffic law for outer space, and who is awarded damages in an accident? At what altitude does outer space begin? Who has legitimate claim to the riches of the earth's mantle, to the minerals at sea bottom? How shall the prospective wealth of Antarctica be divided? What share should the United Nations have in these new riches? And most important of all, how can present principles of international law be expanded to establish a workable structure for world peace—the question to which Grenville Clark gave the last years of his life?

Six or eight years of study in school and college, with perhaps a year or two of graduate work, should give our future leaders opportunity for one or more courses in the above eight subjects. Any one of them, of course, could occupy the lifetime of a devoted specialist. As Father Henle has pointed out, there is no correlation in one's education between tonnage of information and the acquiring of wisdom—unless it be negative. Students are stuffed with too much information, to be regurgitated in examinations and then forgotten. We fill their minds, says Father Henle, with "inert ideas." The education of a modern leader demands dynamic ideas.

The above is a rough and preliminary attempt to answer that young man's question, raised at the beginning of the chapter: "What should I study?" The query was an honest one and demands an honest answer. I have specified eight subjects which, out of the experience of a lifetime, seem to me best fitted to prepare a young man or a young woman for dealing with the effects of technology, as they advance at an exponential rate.

The reader may be able to sharpen this curriculum as the dialogue continues; indeed, it is open season for curricula since Russia's Sputnik circled the earth, to the bewilderment of schoolmen everywhere. It should not be an exclusive syllabus for study; many other subjects in the humanities and sciences should remain. Training for a special skill must also have its place.

Granting a useful curriculum, can leaders so equipped find a path out of the jungle? Leaders will certainly come to the fore in the years ahead and, fortified with knowledge of some sort, try to find a way. I believe the prospects will be better with tools like the above to help them.

The great need now is for leaders who can shape their parties and the nation's politics to the realities of present and future, not past—the realities of affluence, not depression; of stifling urban life, not pastoral yeomanry; the realities of a technology that mocks humanity, and a nuclear nightmare that ridicules ideological evangelism.

Thus Tom Wicker in the *New York Times* calls for a new kind of leadership.

There is also the question of how to study. Here, as a footnote to the curriculum, is a fascinating experiment in teaching science in Nepal, reported by Dart and Pradhan in *Science,* February 10, 1967. Children from 9 to 14, after being instructed in some simple findings of modern science, were interviewed about what they had learned. The typical pattern went like this:

Question: "What makes an earthquake?"

Answer: "The earth is supported on the back of a fish. When the fish is tired he shifts his weight. This shakes the whole earth."

All the children agreed with this "folk" explanation. After a pause, however, another child would speak up: "There is fire at the center of the earth. It seeks to escape and sometimes cracks the earth. This causes an earthquake." All the children then agreed to this "scientific" explanation.

What a light this simple demonstration throws on teaching, human nature, culture, and learning. The children in Nepal— and probably throughout the East—had no difficulty in accepting two widely different explanations of an earthquake, one taught at home, the other at school. Neither included any experimental proof. In school they learned by rote, out of a book; at home they learned by parental authority.

It is only too clear that a curriculum in Nepal—or indeed anywhere else—which relies on memorizing facts about earthquakes, or rainfall, or lightning, will be useless. The authors of this striking experiment conclude that the scientific attitude can be taught only by setting up simple laboratory tests, where children use their hands and eyes, with a strong appeal to the child's innate curiosity.

A FINAL PROPOSAL

In Chapter 13 we mentioned the "Pugwash Conferences," where scientists from all over the world meet to focus the scientific attitude on problems of disarmament, radiation, and the structure of peace. This new and valuable social invention might well be expanded to consider the whole impact of technology. We remember that the seventh point in the scientific attitude, cited on page 211, was the "evaluation of consequences." Along this line the American Association for the Advancement of Science has set up a "Committee for the Promotion of Human Welfare," which reports that technology has been "used with excessive haste and before complete understanding of the full effects"—and notes fallout and insecticides, among other examples. The committee recommends a sharp reduction in existing governmental and commercial secrecy, which blocks the scientific evaluation of large-scale technical innovation.

To go a step further, we need a supranational Bureau of

Standards to screen technological inventions before putting them into mass production, by either industry or government. "All mankind," says the *New York Times*, "can be threatened by unexpected consequences. The need is for worldwide appreciation of the serious warnings now given, and worldwide efforts—perhaps through the United Nations—to meet a worldwide problem."

The *Times* asks whether the race to beat the Russians to the moon is a worthwhile example of government support of science. The spin-off in the form of new knowledge is alleged to be great, but what does it really amount to? Who has taken an impartial inventory? Perhaps the whole NASA operation should be removed from the Rose-Bowl-championship-football class and organized as a sober, careful, probably manless, exploration of space by the United States, Russia, and all high-energy societies, in a joint scientific enterprise under the auspices of the United Nations.

There are plenty of other innovations ripe for screening. High on the list might come the antimissile missile. What will it do in the way of exacerbating the arms race, increasing the danger of war by accident, and what will it cost—$50 billion or $100 billion?

Again, how about biological and chemical warfare, now in active R & D? What can this elaborate mischief-making do to the total human environment and the complex balance of nature? Nobody knows.

Can the supersonic airliner (S.S.T.) really serve a human need on this small planet, while it smashes a 50-mile-wide corridor of sonic boom?

And what promises to be the ultimate effect on the planet's climate of releasing carbon dioxide from industry and motor vehicles at the present rate? One estimate, as noted earlier, is a 4-degree Centigrade increase in world temperature by the year 2000. How soon thereafter will polar ice caps begin to melt, and the oceans to rise?

After more than one million Americans have been killed over the years, some real work is at last being done on building safety, as well as cosmetics, into a motorcar. But the question of motor accidents consists of at least four variables:

The safety of the car

The engineering of the road

The driving environment—signboards, conflicting lights, noise, fog, etc.

The competence of the driver

This is a job for systems analysis. Who is doing it?

The Commission to Study the Organization of Peace issued in 1967 a report drafted by Louis B. Sohn of Harvard. It urged study by the UN of the impact of new technology. It cited the danger of using computers as decision-makers for the military; it cited the proposed data-processing center to keep track of every American, and the expansion of bugging devices to end all privacy. It questioned the proposals of some biologists to change human genes and decide who shall have many children and who shall have none. Indeed, all proposals for remaking Homo sapiens based on breaking the genetic code should be scrutinized with the utmost caution. "Man may be able to program his own cells," says *Science,* "long before he will be able to assess the long-term consequences."

The United Nations might well be the home of such a Bureau of Standards, and the depository for all relevant scientific information on large technological innovations which can seriously affect society.

One could sleep better at night if some such screening bureau were at work in its laboratories and in the field, manned by scientists who were also philosophers. It would give political leaders, furthermore, firm ground on which to stand, and make decisions. The path to knowledge might really begin to open, and the jungle to be pushed back.

EPILOGUE: NOT QUITE UTOPIA

DR. PLATT, we remember, said that the world is now too dangerous for anything short of Utopia. With this encouragement, let us sight along the trend curves. What might be the shape of things to come a generation hence?

If we look back a generation we land in the depths of the Great Depression, with all American banks closed and the unemployment rate at 25 percent. Had you been able to tell a university professor—one who still held his job—what to expect in the generation ahead, he would have thought you mad. He would not have discounted a violent revolution in 1933, for America was not too far from that; but universal social security, vast federal subsidies to farmers, the TVA, the CCC camps, Federal Arts projects, and government insurance for every bank depositor—stuff and nonsense! The Supreme Court would never allow it.

More improbable still in his view would have been Pearl Harbor, Buchenwald, Stalin as brother-in-arms in another world war, the destruction of a great city by a single, small atomic bomb, the population explosion of the 1960's (in 1933 the population *rate* was going down), the race to the moon, computers burrowing into nearly every organized activity.

If a professor in the Depression would have had to stretch his mind uncomfortably to accept the late 1960's we ought to be permitted a little mind-stretching to view the end of the century. So here we go:

A faculty member of the Westchester State College, let us say, walks out to his mailbox for the Sunday *New York Times* on a spring morning in the year 2001. The shad-blow is almost over and the orioles are back. The *Times* weighs just half a pound, rather than the present eight. It is charged to his personal account in the computerized credit system to which every American citizen belongs. His salary is of course credited. Competitive advertising has largely disappeared, leaving chiefly news, reviews and comment.

As he looks up, the sky is a deep, unpolluted blue.

A squirrel is chattering, but he hears no thundering jets, no sonic booms, no grinding trucks, roaring motorcycles, screeching station wagons, or grunting bulldozers.

Along the clear, almost transparent road, faintly luminous at night, comes a fuel-cell car, small, quiet, easy to park, shockproof, fumeless. . . . An electric truck follows. Yellow daffodils are blooming by a roadside innocent of beer cans.

Water from the nuclear desalting plant at Greenwich is cold and free of chlorine, with plenty for lawn, garden, and community swimming pool. Private, unguarded pools are banned —too many children were drowned in this struggle for prestige. The fear of drought has disappeared forever—at least in coastal areas.

There are no commercials on television, a service now charged to citizens in the national credit system along with other public utilities.

The beaches of Long Island Sound are white and clean, and shore birds are thick in the wide salt marshes. Power boats with fuel cells are as silent as the sailboats, and water skiing is assigned a separate area, with stiff penalties for leaving it. The waters of the Sound are clear and clean. Great schools of shad are running up the Hudson and Connecticut rivers, shellfish are healthy and abundant. Even Lake Erie is slowly beginning to breathe again.

Through a gap in his tall pine grove, the professor can see on the horizon the towers of the New Town near White Plains. It is one of a dozen local centers in the New York urban field, helping to take the pressure off Manhattan. Its symphony orchestra, he recalls, won the recent All-American competition.

No private automobiles are now permitted in Manhattan, not even for the grandest politicos. Electric buses, electric trucks for night deliveries, plenty of fuel-cell taxis, bicycles on the special paths constitute the vehicles aboveground. The professor can go from a station near his home to Manhattan in 20 noiseless minutes underground. It takes him no longer to the international airport, where Stol-planes rise and descend vertically with almost no noise. The supersonic liners have been abandoned, pending a solution of the sonic boom problem. The professor can get anywhere in the world comfortably in a few hours, as it is.

A good half of New York City's area is now open space, following the Great Demolition of the 1980's, and population is down to an unhurried five million. No crowds yell at a would-be suicide, "Go ahead and jump!" The parks are safe at night; the malls with their fountains, flowers, and sidewalk cafés are pleasant for shopping or for meditation by day.

The United Nations has left New York for an island of its own in the Indian Ocean. It has a powerful legislative body responsible to no nation but to mankind, and the whole organization is intensively devoted to settling disputes between nations, enforcing disarmament, and balancing the world economy. Its lordly budget of over $100 billion a year comes from royalties on various supranational resources, drawn from the sea, from Antarctica, and from the earth's mantle. A cut in the tolls of the new sea-level canal across Nicaragua also helps.

The last substantial war, beyond UN control, ended in Southeast Asia in the early 1970's, when the governments of both belligerents were overwhelmingly displaced by their exasperated, bereaved, and impoverished citizens, and the UN was called in to mandate the whole devastated area. The explosion of several nuclear weapons on each side was the dreadful price for bringing permanent peace on earth.

The cold war between the U.S. and the U.S.S.R. was finally abandoned in the late 1960's. One reason was that Russian scientists discovered and gave to the world a cure for cancer. The impact even dissolved the John Birch Society.

China and a reunited Germany are now strong supporters of the United Nations. As a result of the steady growth of the mixed economy, the opposing ideologies of Communism and the Radical Right have all but withered away. Mr. William F. Buckley, Jr. devotes his still energetic mind to raising delphiniums.

No human landings on Mars or Venus are now planned. The terrible disaster on the return from the moon by the first astronauts determined that. Outer space is obviously inhospitable for long trips by earthlings; there are too many unknown variables. Exploration is still vigorously carried on, but by unmanned vehicles and instruments, under the direction of scientists in UNESCO.

Competition between nations is largely confined to advances in the arts, research, and the Olympic Games. Deprived of its military function, a nation is now a nostalgic homeland, and a much more decent and friendly institution. Capital punishment has been abolished in most countries, the crime rate is down, and there is no point to stealing money in a society devoted to computerized credit.

Every child on earth now learns the world language—with its phonetic spelling and simple structure—through television lessons and plays. A little fiction and poetry have recently been written in this synthetic tongue, but its literary value remains to be proved, however excellent it may be for international conferences.

Nearly every child on earth receives all the education his genes permit. He grows up an independent thinker, informed by the scientific attitude. This has gone far to heal race relations, but no final solution can yet be announced. There is however, no *Apartheid* in South Africa and no "Black Power" in the United States.

The American population is growing at half of one percent a year, down from 1.6 percent in 1965. The world rate stands at 0.7 percent. Though birth control is universally available, with some extraordinary new techniques in both sterilization and tranquilizing the sex drive, these growth rates are known to be too high. Planetary policy aims at a rate of *zero* by 2025, with world population thereafter never to exceed seven billion children, women, and men. That seems to be the maximum our living space can comfortably support. It is no longer a question of the food supply setting the total, but elbow room.

The food supply in calories is now growing at 1.3 percent, almost twice the rate of population. Some African children are still undernourished, but the dreadful famines of the 1970's and 1980's will never come again, and the insidious and deadly new variety of plague which then originated to balance births with deaths has at last been conquered by the World Health Organization.

Nuclear power plants, using the fusion process with hydrogen from all the oceans as raw material, are now beginning to raise living standards everywhere, and the area once known as the Hungry World—two-thirds of mankind—has lost its title. The battle now is with the temptations of material abundance rather than with the deprivations of scarcity. Economic textbooks are at last being rewritten on this principle.

Our professor walks back from his pleasant roadside, waving to a neighbor on horseback, hacking along the parallel trail. He breathes deep of the fresh spring air, notes the dogwood buds almost ready to create their annual snowdrift, and enters his pleasant home, warmed and serviced by wireless pulsations of energy. He opens the Sunday *Times* to read the latest instrument analysis from Mars. Yes, once there were probably living creatures on Mars, and then . . . ?

READING LIST

Abrams, Charles, *Man's Struggle for Shelter*. Cambridge: MIT Press, 1964.

Beaton, Leonard, *The Struggle for Peace*. New York: Praeger, 1966.

Berelson, B., and Steiner, G. A., *Human Behavior*. New York: Harcourt, Brace & World, 1964.

Blackett, P. M. S., *Studies of War*. New York: Hill & Wang, 1962.

Blake, Peter, *God's Own Junkyard*. New York: Holt, Rinehart & Winston, 1964.

Brown, Harrison, *The Challenge of Man's Future*. New York: Viking Press, 1963.

Brown, Harrison, and others, *The Next Hundred Years*. New York: Viking Press, 1957.

Carr, Donald E., *The Breath of Life: The Problem of Poisoned Air*. New York: W. W. Norton, 1965.

Chase, Stuart, *The Proper Study of Mankind* (revised edition). New York: Harper & Row, 1956. (Chapter I deals with the scientific method.)

Chase, Stuart, *Rich Land, Poor Land*. New York: Whittlesey House, 1936.

Clark, Grenville, and Sohn, Louis B., *World Peace Through World Law*. Cambridge: Harvard University Press, 1960.

Clarke, Arthur C., *Profiles of the Future*. New York: Harper & Row, 1962.

232   READING LIST

Cohen, Benjamin V., *The United Nations*. Cambridge: Harvard University Press, 1961.

Commoner, Barry, *Science and Survival*. New York: Viking Press, 1966.

Cornelius, David K., and St. Vincent, Edwin, eds., *Cultures in Conflict: Perspectives on the Snow-Leavis Controversy*. Chicago: Scott, Foresman, 1964.

Cousins, Norman, *In Place of Folly*. New York: Harper & Brothers, 1961.

Crutchfield, Richard S., and others, *New Approaches to Individualizing Instruction*. Princeton: Educational Testing Service, 1965.

Dollard, John; Doob, Leonard; and others, *Frustration and Aggression*. New Haven: Yale University Press, 1939.

Ellul, Jacques, *The Technological Society,* translated from the French by John Wilkinson. New York: Alfred A. Knopf, 1964.

Galbraith, John Kenneth, *The Affluent Society*. Boston: Houghton Mifflin, 1958.

Galbraith, John Kenneth, *The New Industrial State*. Boston: Houghton Mifflin, 1967.

Holland, Laurence, ed., *Who Designs America?* New York: Doubleday Anchor Books, 1966.

Huxley, Aldous, *Brave New World*. New York: Harper & Brothers, 1932.

Huxley, Aldous, *Brave New World Revisited*. New York: Harper & Brothers, 1958.

Kennan, George F., *On Dealing with the Communist World*. New York: Harper & Row, 1964.

Kennan, George F., *Russia and the West*. Boston: Little, Brown, 1961.

Keynes, John Maynard, *The General Theory of Employment, Interest and Money*. New York: Harcourt, Brace, 1936.

Keys, Donald, *God and the H-Bomb*. New York: Macfadden Books, 1961. (Symposium of churchmen.)

Kroeber, Theodora, *Ishi*. Berkeley: University of California Press, 1965.

Lapp, Ralph E., *Kill and Overkill*. New York: Basic Books, 1963.

Lapp, Ralph E., *The New Priesthood*. New York: Harper & Row, 1965.

Larson, Arthur, *A Warless World*. New York: McGraw-Hill, 1963. (Symposium by Toynbee, Millis, Boulding, Mead, Hocking and others.)

Lorenz, Konrad, *On Aggression*. New York: Harcourt, Brace & World, 1966.

Lowe, Jeanne R., *Cities in a Race with Time*. New York: Random House, 1967.

Lyford, Joseph P., *The Airtight Cage*. New York: Harper & Row, 1965.

Mead, Margaret, *Continuities in Cultural Evolution*. New Haven: Yale University Press, 1964.

Millis, Walter, *An End to Arms*. New York: Atheneum, 1965.

Millis, Walter, and Real, James, *The Abolition of War*. New York: Macmillan, 1963.

Morse, Dean, and Warner, A. W., eds., *Technological Innovation and Society*. New York: Columbia University Press, 1966. (A symposium.)

National Commission on Technology, Automation and Economic Progress: *Report to President and Congress*. Washington, D.C.: U.S. Government Printing Office, 1966.

Newman, James R., *The Rule of Folly*. New York: Simon & Schuster, 1962.

Oppenheimer, Robert, and others, *The Scientific Endeavor*. New York: Rockefeller Institute Press, 1965.

Orwell, George, *1984*. New York: Harcourt, Brace, 1949.

Platt, John R., *The Step to Man*. New York: John Wiley & Sons, 1966.

Population Bulletin. Published 8 times a year by Population Reference Bureau, Inc., Washington, D.C.

Schlivek, Louis B., *Man in Metropolis*. New York: Doubleday, 1965.

Scott, John, *Democracy Is Not Enough*. New York: Harcourt, Brace, 1960.

Shannon, Claude, and Weaver, Warren, *The Mathematical Theory of Communication*. Urbana: University of Illinois Press, 1949.

Shotwell, James T., *The Faith of an Historian*. New York: Walker & Company, 1964.

Smith, Alice Kimball, *A Peril and a Hope*. Chicago: University of Chicago Press, 1965. (Scientists and nuclear war, 1945-47.)

Snow, C. P., *The Two Cultures and the Scientific Revolution*. London: Cambridge University Press, 1959.

Snow, C. P., *Variety of Men*. New York: Charles Scribner's Sons, 1967. (Chapters on Einstein, Churchill, Hammarskjöld, and Stalin.)

Stapledon, W. Olaf, *Last and First Men*. New York: Jonathan Cape & Harrison Smith, 1931.

Szent-Gyorgi, Albert, *Science, Ethics and Politics*. New York: Vanguard Press, 1964.

Udall, Stewart L., *The Quiet Crisis*. New York: Holt, Rinehart & Winston, 1965.

Union of International Agencies, *Year Book, Brussels*. (French and English.)

Walker, Charles R., and Guest, Robert H., *The Man on the Assembly Line*. Cambridge: Harvard University Press. 1952.

Warburg, James P., *Time for Statesmanship*. New York: Current Affairs Press, 1965.

Wiener, Norbert, *The Human Use of Human Beings*. Boston: Houghton Mifflin, 1950.

Wiesner, Jerome B., *Where Science and Politics Meet*. New York: McGraw-Hill, 1965. (Includes a joint paper with Dr. Herbert F. York.)

INDEX